"Worldwide human trafficking is a modern form of slavery that negates justice and neighbor-love in the worst possible way. From Korea now comes a prophetic call to the church to move realistically to counter it. God give us ears to hear Eddie Byun's word for our times."

J. I. Packer, professor of theology, Regent College

"Everyone loves the idea of justice—until there's a cost. But the truth is there's always a cost to justice. Pastor Eddie calls the church to pursue justice not because it's trendy, but because God loves justice and hates injustice. This book walks us through the path of seeking justice."

Eugene Cho, pastor of Quest Church and founder of One Day's Wages

"*Justice Awakening* is a wake-up call for the church to rise up and take her rightful place on the frontlines in the fight for freedom and justice for the oppressed. This book beats with the passionate heart of God and gives practical ways for us to be the hands of God to those who are enslaved. We need more books like this to equip and inspire the church. May the church respond with courageous obedience and lead the fight to end human trafficking and modern-day slavery."

Mike Bickle, director of the International House of Prayer of Kansas City

"*Justice Awakening* calls us to look at the dark places in our neighborhoods we would rather turn our eyes from. In the midst of growing our churches or the busyness of our programs, Eddie Byun reminds us of our responsibility to be a community of light and uncomfortable love. *Justice Awakening* is a plea to the church to love boldly and to love now!"

Dave Gibbons, founder/CVO of Xealots.org

"Whether your church wants to be educated about human trafficking, gain a biblical perspective concerning it or seek practical means to combat the evil, *Justice Awakening* is a must-read. Pastor Eddie's church is on the cutting edge of fighting human trafficking, and in this book he gives the church proven methods to answer God's command to stand with the oppressed and fight injustice."

Don Brewster, founder and director of Agape International Missions

"Fighting human trafficking is one of the greatest challenges of our generation. But where should churches start if they want to make a difference? Pastor Eddie Byun lays out not only the biblical mandate of bringing justice to the oppressed, but he also describes both spiritual and practical ways that a church can help. *Justice Awakening* is an essential resource for any church leader who wants to bring hope and justice to those ensnared in human trafficking."

D. Michael Lindsay, president of Gordon College and author of *Faith in the Halls of Power*

"This is a great book! Pastor Eddie reminds us of the biblical standard for justice, but he doesn't leave us there, lest we become self-righteous. He brings to light the complex issues that fuel the trade, but he doesn't leave us there, lest we become puffed up with knowledge. He challenges us to involvement, but he doesn't leave us there, lest we feel overwhelmed. This book is a timely wake-up call for the church to actively engage in the fight against human trafficking and the release of prisoners from its darkness."

Annie Dieselberg, founder and CEO of NightLight International

"Pastor Eddie Byun couldn't be any clearer in his message to the church. The church needs to be relevant, and a key to their relevance is to be leaders in the fight against modern-day slavery. That's loving your neighbor as yourself, and that is the heart of Jesus!"

Jeremy Affeldt, pitcher for the San Francisco Giants and author of *To Stir a Movement*

"What I love about this book is seeing Pastor Eddie's passion for justice, which flows powerfully from God's heart for justice. I say 'Amen!' to his challenge for the church to be the ones leading the way to bringing an end to this injustice. It's not enough to be aware of this issue—it's a call from the heart of God to take action and to help abolish slavery in our lifetime."

Michael Oh, executive director and CEO, Lausanne Movement

"Pastor Eddie's passion for God and for justice is contagious. Eddie has dedicated his life to the abolition of human trafficking and oppression. His book is both visionary and practical, calling the church to fulfill its mission to care for the oppressed, the downtrodden and the forgotten. This is an important and life-altering book."

Trace Bundy, instrumental acoustic guitarist

"This is a fantastic resource for the church! The biblical narrative makes it clear that worship without justice is a stench in the face of God. At a time when there is more slavery than ever before in history, Pastor Eddie calls the church to engage in the fight to set people free from everything that enslaves them. His words are timely, powerful and echo the very heart cry of God."

Daniel Walker, author of *God in a Brothel*

"I was deeply convicted reading Pastor Eddie's words: 'Trafficking today is one of the darkest evils in existence. . . . The reason why it has become so enormous globally is because the church has ignored it and avoided this dark evil for far too long. It is time for that to change, beginning today.' This statement says it all. Christians need to read this book, wake up and start getting involved for change."

David Sang-Bok Kim, president of Torch Trinity Graduate University

"Tears of passion and resolve flowed from my eyes as I read *Justice Awakening*. This important book articulates the way our heavenly Father teaches and inspires us to reveal what's in his heart. It resonates within us to press on as we fight to find and free slaves. This book is a critical journey through God's direct instructions to the church about justice and human trafficking. Thank you, Pastor Eddie, for crafting such a great tool for the body of Christ!"

Carol Hart, cofounder and president of ZOE International

"If you need a biblically sound, well-researched and balanced treatment of the growing justice movement, this is it! Pastor Eddie Byun captures the issues clearly, refuses to compromise on the gospel, and provides practical and wise words of implementation to turn good intentions into life-changing impact. I ministered personally with Pastor Eddie in Korea and am honored and thrilled to recommend him and this excellent work to you."

Chip Ingram, senior pastor of Venture Christian Church and CEO of Living on the Edge Ministries

"I highly recommend this book for the church today. Its message is needed for our generation. Pastor Eddie is someone that I deeply love and respect, and this book is a gift."

Young-Gil Kim, president of Handong Global University

"Sex trafficking is the new form of slavery in our time. Pastor Eddie Byun exposes this brutal evil and gives a biblical call to justice and practical steps for the church—God's instrument for healing and justice in our broken world."

Dennis P. Hollinger, president, Gordon-Conwell Theological Seminary

"So often when faced with the overwhelming evil of human trafficking we feel helpless and wonder what we can do. Pastor Eddie provides not only a striking biblical demand for action but also the tools by which we can take those first steps and through which the lives of both the reader and the oppressed can be transformed. The embers of justice smolder quietly within the church. They are largely domesticated and frequently lack expression. This book is gasoline!"

Brian McConaghy, founder and director, Ratanak International

"This book tells a story of God's justice being done on the earth, showing hope that human trafficking can be stopped by a church who gains his heart for the oppressed. *Justice Awakening* contains many practical steps that can help the church to change the world and end modern-day slavery."

Philip Choi, Bank of Korea

"*Justice Awakening* provides both the blueprints and the foundation for the church to 'rise up' and build an effective, God-focused justice ministry to end human trafficking. It educates and encourages, confronts and challenges—and then provides practical, down-to-earth, doable action steps. This book is a gift to the antitrafficking movement. Thank you, Pastor Eddie, for this much-needed resource."

Becca C. Johnson, director of US aftercare, Agape International Mission (AIM)

"Eddie Byun has dedicated himself to working for the righteousness of God's kingdom in turning the tide against the evil and injustices in Korea's society, in particular sex trafficking, which the Korean church has been neglecting. I consider *Justice Awakening* a blessing from the Lord. I sincerely pray that, through this book, many Christians will come to join this fight and bring freedom and justice in our generation."

Rev. Joshua Jae-Hoon Lee, senior pastor of Onnuri Community Church, Seoul

JUSTICE
AWAKENING

How You and Your Church Can
Help End Human Trafficking

EDDIE BYUN

IVP Books

An imprint of InterVarsity Press
Downers Grove, Illinois

InterVarsity Press
P.O. Box 1400, Downers Grove, IL 60515-1426
World Wide Web: www.ivpress.com
Email: email@ivpress.com

InterVarsity Press® is the book-publishing division of InterVarsity Christian Fellowship/USA®,
a movement of students and faculty active on campus at hundreds of universities, colleges and
schools of nursing in the United States of America, and a member movement of the
International Fellowship of Evangelical Students. For information about local and regional
activities, write Public Relations Dept., InterVarsity Christian Fellowship/USA, 6400 Schroeder
Rd., P.O. Box 7895, Madison, WI 53707-7895, or visit the IVCF website at www.intervarsity.org.

Cover design: Cindy Kiple
Interior design: Beth Hagenberg

Images: heart-shaped paper: melhi/Getty Images
       old card: © abzee/iStockphoto
       textured background: © javarman3/iStockphoto

ISBN 978-0-8308-4419-7 (print)
ISBN 978-0-8308-9589-2 (digital)

Printed in the United States of America ∞

Library of Congress Cataloging-in-Publication Data
A catalog record for this book is available from the Library of Congress.

P	16	15	14	13	12	11	10	9	8	7	6	5	4	3	2	1
Y	27	26	25	24	23	22	21	20	19	18	17	16	15	14		

To my Lord and Savior Jesus Christ
who set this captive free from the greatest bondage of all.

To my beautiful wife, Hyun.
I love you so much, and my love for you grows each day.
You are wonderful.

To my daughter, Emma, who is in the presence of Jesus.
I can't wait to see you again.

To my son, Enoch Justus.
I am so happy for the gift you are to me.
I thank God for you each and every day.

CONTENTS

INTRODUCTION

My Journey

Learn to do good;
seek justice,
correct oppression;
bring justice to the fatherless,
plead the widow's cause.

Isaiah 1:17

There are more than 30 million
slaves in the world today.

David Batstone, *Not for Sale*

Nothing in the world is more dangerous
than sincere ignorance and conscientious stupidity.

Martin Luther King Jr.

A HOLY DISCONTENT

My heart was unusually restless. It was late afternoon in Seoul, and outside the sun was already low in the sky. Traffic would be starting the evening crawl. I had been a pastor for over fourteen years (in the US, Canada, Australia and now currently in South Korea) and loved what God had called me to do. I loved the preaching. I loved the discipleship. I loved the shepherding of the flock that was under my care. I loved sharing the gospel with those who did not know Jesus. But for some reason, in the summer of 2010, I just couldn't shake a holy discontent that was lingering in my heart. I felt like there was something else God wanted me to do, but I just couldn't put my finger on it. I spent time in prayer asking God why I was feeling this way. Did God want me to move to a different city? Did God want me to change occupations? Did God want us to change the way we were doing ministry? I wasn't sure, but I definitely knew things weren't supposed to stay the same.

Summer turned to fall. I continued to seek the Lord in prayer, but the restlessness of that evening continued to bother me. I didn't know why. Then, one day, God gave me a word—two words actually—"community transformation." I had no idea what that meant. Did God want me to evangelize more? Were we supposed to serve our neighborhood more? What exactly did "community transformation" mean? I sought the Lord for more clarity, but didn't receive any other instruction—at least not at that time. For the next few months, I had the words "community transformation" in my prayer journal, but didn't know how to continue on from there. If God wasn't going to give me any more information, I just had to trust that he would show me at the right time.

AWAKENING

Each year, our ministry has a theme for that particular year. As 2010 was coming to a close, the theme God gave us for 2011 was "Freedom." Just as I wasn't quite sure what "community transformation" meant for us, I wasn't sure what "freedom" would mean for our ministry either. Maybe God wanted us to experience personal breakthroughs or deliverance from addictions in our lives. Or maybe it would mean that many people would come to know Christ next year and be set free from their sins. Regardless, I was excited to see how the new year would unfold.

In November of 2010, as our church was getting ready to celebrate Thanksgiving, I was given a copy of the book *Not for Sale* by David Batstone, which was my first introduction to human trafficking and modern-day slavery. Up until that point, I had no idea slavery still existed in the world. I had heard of drug trafficking and arms trafficking but not human trafficking. More out of curiosity than anything else, I opened up that book on a cold November evening, and for the next few hours my world was rocked.

Shock! Anger! Rage! My hands tightened as I gripped the

pages of the book. I could not believe what I was reading. I
still remember the emotions that boiled up as I read about the
plight of millions around the world who were bought and
sold as commodities, denied their rights, dignity and honor
as human beings. Young girls in Thailand whose innocence
was stolen from them as men would violate them ten to
twenty times a night. Boys in Uganda who were forced to kill
their own parents and fight in wars instead of playing with
friends and going to school.

The reality struck me like a thunderbolt. For the first time
since that restless visitation, it became clear what God was
trying to say. I had prayed for discernment, for an answer. Now
I had it. The words "community transformation" and "freedom"
all came together in light of what I just read about the evil of
modern-day slavery. Finally, I had a direction to focus all the
restlessness, the holy discontent, that God had placed in me.

Almost every country in the world is stained by the evil of
modern-day slavery. To top it all off, there are millions of
victims around the world. Millions! I shook my head in disbelief. How could so much evil and injustice be going on in
the world and yet I had never heard of any of it?

Every eight seconds someone is sold into slavery. Up to
thirty million people are in slavery around the world. The US
State Department estimates that there are 600,000 to 800,000
children, women and men trafficked across international
borders annually. One study estimates that in South Korea
alone, over one million women have been forced into sexual

servitude. This is a multi-billion dollar industry that affects every nation in the world. The world of human trafficking is very well networked, from law enforcement to immigration to travel agents to taxi drivers.

What drives the demand in the sex trafficking industry? In short, *lust* and *greed*. The lust of the flesh that is so self-centered and so uncontrollable that the customers, or "johns," have become slaves to their own passions. And the greed of the traffickers whose love for money has blinded them to the dignity and honor of a human life. Greed ultimately lures the trafficker into the evil of selling people as property. The uncontrollable appetite for more wealth has destroyed the conscience of the trafficker, preventing them from seeing the true dignity of a human life.

Scripture warns us of the corrupting dangers of greed:

For the love of money is a root of all kinds of evils. (1 Timothy 6:10)

You shall not pervert justice. You shall not show partiality, and you shall not accept a bribe, for a bribe blinds the eyes of the wise and subverts the cause of the righteous. (Deuteronomy 16:19)

Human trafficking is sin manifesting itself in one of its darkest forms. If you hear the stories of these women and children who have endured starvation, rape, physical beatings, mental manipulation, poor living conditions, and having their lives, dreams and dignity stolen away from them, then you realize that what has happened to these precious souls is nothing short of pure evil. For many, the life they've endured as a slave is the closest thing to hell on earth anyone can experience.

That is the thing about this evil—we can't see it for what it really is. Evil would like to leave us in the dark, blind to injustice. But when we step back and see the scope to which modern-day slavery has spread to almost every country in the world, we are forced to see it for what it really is. It is huge, systemically global and pervasive, and it is truly evil.

And that is how God defines injustice in his Word. He calls it evil.

> You shall not spread a false report. You shall not join hands with a wicked man to be a malicious witness. You shall not fall in with the many to do evil, nor shall you bear witness in a lawsuit, siding with the many, so as to pervert justice, nor shall you be partial to a poor man in his lawsuit. (Exodus 23:1-3)

Injustice is evil in the sight of God, and I was seeing it in one of its worst forms.

I set the book down on my desk. The stories had shaken me to my core, and my blood was boiling. I was outraged and I knew I had to do something. But what? As a pastor, I started to wonder what my congregation could do. I did an online search to find churches that had ministries combating trafficking so that I could get my church on board. Unfortunately, my search came up empty. Many churches had ministries to serve the poor and to help the orphans of the world, but I couldn't find a ministry that was trying to bring an end to human trafficking in our day. Regardless, I knew without a shadow of a doubt that we as a church had to do something.

With no precedent before me and with no books on "how the church can fight human trafficking" to guide me, I got on my knees and prayed once again, "God, I am so angry at all the injustices that I just read about. I cannot believe this is happening, and I know your heart breaks too. God, what can I do? What can our church do? Guide us, lead us, and use us for your glory to bring forth justice in our day."

As I prayed, I also kept a pen and pad of paper next to me. One of the things I like to do is brainstorm with God. I pray and wait for God to speak. I leave room for God to give me inspiration, ideas and insights on Scripture and on anything that he would have me do. That night, the ideas started to flow.

A CHURCH AWAKENING

With each new idea that God gave me, my heart pounded faster with excitement from the realization that I finally had a game plan to attack this evil. By the end of the year, a passion for justice was burning in my heart, but this was not yet on the radar for my church. I had an action plan but no one to join me in this battle—yet. So at the start of the new year of "freedom," I began preaching on God's heart for justice and the plight of millions in slavery, both physically and spiritually, around the world. We started a new ministry called HOPE Be Restored (HBR) and began monthly meetings where we would pray, learn, strategize and plan our next steps toward justice. We hosted two conferences that first year to educate and equip our people as to what was happening and what we could do to stop it.

In the summer and winter breaks, we sent out short-term mission teams to Thailand and Cambodia to partner with local agencies that were on the frontlines of rescuing children and helping to restore dignity back into their lives. We would pray and fast for weeks at a time and raise money to donate to various anti-human trafficking organizations. Suddenly, this fire for justice spread throughout our church and an army began to rise up.

One of our members whose heart was ignited was Jonathan English. Originally from Texas, Jonathan had come to South Korea to teach English several years earlier. After spending a few years sensing something inside, he found himself—like me—feeling restless and discontented. He knew about justice, had heard of organizations like International Justice Mission (IJM) and would think about it, but it didn't catch fire in him until one day he found himself praying, "God, I don't know what it is, but I want to get my hands dirty so that they're caked with mud. I want my shoulders to be sore from lifting people up."

When I began to preach on God's heart for justice, Jonathan said that after listening to the first few sermons, he felt God speaking to him as the psalmist in Psalm 10 cries out for help for those who are oppressed by the wicked. Suddenly, it hit him: "You are there to help! You are someone who does not turn and hide from the afflicted! You are the one called to help those in need!" Then, fired up by our first freedom and justice conference, Jonathan actively made connections with Eco-Gender, a group dedicated to rescuing sex trafficked women in Korea. During EcoGender's annual conference, he went to an area called Paju, which is north of Seoul, and cooked lunch for the staff for a week. Jonathan has since served as the assistant director for HOPE Be Restored and has been relentless in his service to EcoGender. He is just one example of the fire that was lit within our congregation.

Soon, others began to rise up. I encouraged our congregation—many of them expats and foreign teachers—not to simply return to their home countries once their contracts were over, but to consider working in countries where sex trafficking occurred and where the presence of the church was in greater need. One of our members, Elizabeth Lee, stepped up and heeded the call. She decided to devote herself to work in Northern Thailand with a group called Zoe that rescues and restores children who were sold into the sex industry. She said, "I was already planning on leaving for missions . . . but hearing Pastor Eddie's sermon on missions and justice gave me more courage to make my decision. Then, after another short-term trip with our church to Thailand in the summer of 2010, Pastor Eddie preached a sermon titled 'Finishing the Mission' that helped me take that step into the mission field to care for those trapped in injustice. That short-term trip was a time of confirmation for me to move to Thailand." Needless to say our congregation was incredibly excited to send Elizabeth to Thailand in the fall of 2012.

Even one of our own administrative staff, Buri—a very sweet, cheery woman—suddenly became a courageous warrior, enflamed with a passion for justice before our very eyes. After meeting orphans rescued from the sex trade in Thailand, her life was forever changed. She eventually left our staff to also pursue full-time work with human trafficking victims.

So many of us had been moved to tears, so many of us had been convicted by the stunning and spine-chilling plight of children and women in the throes of evil, and so many of us had been touched by God's heart for his most precious and vulnerable people. We had been sleeping before, but as we began to put our faith into action, an army was waking up in our congregation. It was a beautiful sight to behold.

A YEAR OF FREEDOM

Everything became clearer with each step we took. I now understood what God meant by giving our church the words "community transformation." He was letting us know that the upcoming ministry year would be a year of "freedom." God wanted us to enter into the fight for freedom and combat the great evil of human trafficking in our community and around the world as a church.

As the year progressed, it truly became a year of freedom on so many levels. Our timing seemed to hit a wave sweeping the world. Other organizations and churches seemed to be experiencing a growing of awareness on this issue as well. Laws were being passed as the government made gestures toward cracking down on sex trafficking. Just as we were getting the social justice ball rolling in 2011, CNN announced The Freedom Project, promising to spotlight more stories on fighting human slavery. Although they were a secular news organization, they made me reflect on the role of the church in partnering with the cause (I talk more about this later). CNN even shot footage of our Freedom Sunday service in Seoul.

Meanwhile, churches and ministries in the States, such as the Passion Conference in Atlanta, led by Louie Giglio, announced their commitment to ending modern-day slavery. We later networked with International House of Prayer (IHOP), Agape International Missions (AIM) in Cambodia, International Justice Mission (IJM), and Not for Sale to build a stronger international network of partnerships. Within Korea, we expanded our ministries to include single mothers and orphans because they were some of the most vulnerable groups to trafficking. The international premier of the documentary *Nefarious: Merchant of Souls,* a powerful film that uncovers the global sex trade, directed by Benjamin Nolot of Exodus Cry, was held at our church as we began screening tours across the country.

Not only were we helping to free people who were once in slavery in Korea and around the world, our church was also being set free to truly be the living body of Christ that it was meant to be. Our church was coming alive to a degree that I had never seen before. We were caring for the outcast and giving up our own food and money so that the poor might be fed. We were no longer focused on ourselves, but on loving our neighbors as God intended his people to do. The transformation was enormous, and with it came new challenges, including some resistance. But overall, the momentum was too great to deny. This is where God was leading us.

WHAT CAN WE DO TO HELP?

Though we had our share of critics, that was thankfully not the case with most of the churches and pastors I would come across. In fact, as more people found out about what we were doing, the number one question I heard was, "What can my church do to help?"

Time and time again, the biggest frustration I would see in others was not knowing what they could do to enter this fight for freedom and justice around the world. Beyond just giving money to other organizations—as good as that was—the question that kept coming up was, "What could an individual or a church do to end human trafficking in our day?"

Fortunately, my brainstorming sessions with God gave me a number of practical steps to recommend to people. This is one of the main reasons I wrote this book. I want to provide the masses with practical ideas for every person to become a part of the solution to this problem. Whatever your gifting is, use it to send a message to your sphere of influence. Whatever your passion is, use it to spread this message of justice for all. So write, paint, draw, speak, publish, compose, act, campaign and do anything else to the glory of God and for the freedom of all people.

I want to help individual believers and their church communities rise up and become an influence of change for the good of our cities and communities around the world. It is my prayer that the fruit of this book will result in the freedom of the nations. And who knows, maybe even the freedom of some churches along the way as well.

GROUP DISCUSSION QUESTIONS

- When did you first hear about human trafficking, and how did it make you feel?
- What do you know about human trafficking in your own community?
- Do you feel the church should be involved for freedom and justice around the world? Why or why not?

PRAYER GUIDE

- Ask God to give you his heart of love, compassion and justice as you read this book.
- Pray for your church to be a source of light and love to the community that you are in.
- Pray that the fruit of this study will lead to freedom in your nation.

GOD'S PASSION FOR JUSTICE
IN HIS WORD

But let justice roll down like waters,
and righteousness like an ever-flowing stream.

Amos 5:24

More than 300,000 children younger than age 18 are
trafficked to serve in armed conflicts worldwide.

UNICEF

So enormous, so dreadful, so irremediable did the (slave) trade's
wickedness appear that my own mind was completely made up
for abolition. Let the consequences be what they would,
I from this time determined that I would never
rest until I had effected its abolition.

William Wilberforce

The word *justice* has been used in the press quite often in recent days. In 2011, huge crowds of protesters gathered in major cities across the United States chanting slogans and holding signs of outrage demanding economic justice during the Occupy Wall Street movement. Also in the same year, a course on justice by Harvard professor Michael Sandel proved to be so popular that PBS did a twelve-series special, which spiraled into a national best-selling book and speaking tours, including a sold-out lecture in South Korea. In case after case, we can see outrage, emotion and debate sparked by tragic grievances in all avenues and scales of society— from corrupt officials, displaced auto workers, wrongly convicted inmates, workplace firings—all clamoring for justice.

The concept of justice is not just for mature adults to comprehend. It is deep within us even as children who fully understand the concept of fairness. If you have two young children and give one child five cookies and the other just one cookie, the child with one cookie will say, "That's not fair!" Or if you tell one child she can play outside and have the other work on homework, the second one will naturally cry out, "But that's not fair!" Children have an innate understanding of justice deep within their souls because our God is a God of justice and we are all made in his image. In his book *Mere Christianity*, C. S. Lewis pointed out that all these notions of fairness and right and wrong ultimately point to a moral law and a moral lawgiver—God. Thus, notions of justice won't go away.

We may have a general understanding of right and wrong from the time we are young, but what is the biblical way to understand justice? That's what we will explore in this chapter.

GOD'S DEFINITION OF JUSTICE

What is God's definition of justice? The word for "justice" in Hebrew is *mishpat,* and it occurs more than two hundred times in the Bible in its various forms. The most basic meaning is "to treat people well,"[1] but it also carries the meaning of giving people what is due them, be it protection or punishment.[2] And the word for justice in the Greek is *dikaiosyne,* which is most commonly translated as "righteousness." So treating people "rightly" or "righteously" is the essence of justice. It is right living in the context of community. Justice and righteousness are closely linked throughout Scripture. They are so essential to God's kingdom that Psalm 89:14 even tells us that righteousness and justice are the foundation of God's throne.

Another way to see justice is the right use of power. Gary Haugen, the founder of International Justice Mission, says: "Justice occurs on earth when power and authority between people is exercised in conformity with God's standards of moral excellence."[3] Simplifying it even further, Tim Keller says that "justice is care for the vulnerable."[4] When people use power and authority to protect, provide, bless and love our neighbor, justice exists within a society. Thus, Scripture often describes justice as caring for the vulnerable in our communities—the poor, the widow, the fatherless and the foreigner.

A primary manifestation of justice is caring for the outcast and oppressed within society. And to care for them means to meet their deepest needs. Are they hungry? Feed them. Are they naked? Clothe them. Are they oppressed? Set them free. Are they fearful? Protect them in such a way as to relieve them of their fears. When we care for the vulnerable in our communities, we are establishing justice in the eyes of God. To God, justice is caring for the poor: "You shall not pervert the justice due to your poor in his lawsuit" (Exodus 23:6). It is caring for the fatherless, the widow and the sojourner.

> You shall not pervert the justice due to the sojourner or to the fatherless, or take a widow's garment in pledge. (Deuteronomy 24:17)

> "Cursed be anyone who perverts the justice due to the sojourner, the fatherless, and the widow." And all the people shall say, "Amen." (Deuteronomy 27:19)

And who were the fatherless, the widow and the sojourner of their day? They were the most vulnerable people within their society. So we see that God places a high value on the poor and oppressed within our society. To God, if they are vulnerable, they are valuable. And to care for them, protect them and provide for them is to establish justice in our land.

If justice is the right use of power, then injustice is an abuse of power, when power is not used in a way that matches the excellence of God's morality. Injustice in society is "taking advantage of those who have little or no economic or social power."[5] Haugen says, "Injustice occurs when power is misused to take from others what God has given them, namely, their life, dignity, liberty or the fruits of their love and labor." It is about the strong abusing, taking advantage of and preying on the weak. When people no longer care for the weak, the poor and the vulnerable, injustice will spread like a plague throughout society.

Although I grew up in the church, I rarely heard anything about God's heart for justice. But as I began to study this topic, I saw this theme saturated throughout Scripture. So if you're like me, maybe you also thought justice wasn't that big of a deal to our Christian faith. Let's take a journey through Scripture to see just how passionate God's heart is for justice.

OUR GOD OF JUSTICE

Our God is a God of justice. Our pursuit of justice must begin with a pursuit of God, because a foundational attribute of God is that he is a God of justice. It is the essence of who he is and the core of his being. So we begin with God. Justice is God's design. Justice is God's desire. Justice is God's passion that beats within his heart. Our mighty God is a God of justice.

Therefore the LORD waits to be gracious to you,
    and therefore he exalts himself to show mercy to
    you.
For the LORD is a God of justice;
    blessed are all those who wait for him.
      (Isaiah 30:18, emphasis added)

The overflow of all that God does is from the place of justice, for all his ways are just.

The Rock, his work is perfect,
    for all his ways are justice.
A God of faithfulness and without iniquity,
    just and upright is he. (Deuteronomy 32:4,
      emphasis added)

To know the ways of the Lord is to know the justice of God. Scripture says that the great and the wise know this about our God—that he is just.

Then I said, "These are only the poor;
    they have no sense;
for they do not know the way of the LORD,
    the justice of their God.
I will go to the great
    and will speak to them,
for they know the way of the LORD,
    the justice of their God." (Jeremiah 5:4-5, emphasis
      added)

Justice comes from the Lord. Our hearts cry out for justice. So where do we turn? We turn to God, because God is the ultimate source of all justice. Every form of government we have seen throughout human history has proven that no one leader or type of government can truly establish justice in all the earth. The ultimate solution to the problem of injustice is found in Christ.

> Many seek the face of a ruler,
>> but it is from the LORD that a man gets justice.
>> (Proverbs 29:26)

God gives wisdom so that justice might be done. When just decisions are made, it is God who has blessed that person with the wisdom to make the right choice.

> And all Israel heard of the judgment that the king had rendered, and they stood in awe of the king, because they perceived that the wisdom of God was in him to do justice. (1 Kings 3:28)

In speaking of the coming Messiah, Isaish says the Lord Jesus is the one through whom justice will finally be established over all the earth. The mission of the Messiah is to bring forth justice to all the nations of the earth.

> Behold my servant, whom I uphold,
>> my chosen, in whom my soul delights;
> I have put my Spirit upon him;

he will bring forth justice to the nations.
He will not cry aloud or lift up his voice,
    or make it heard in the street;
a bruised reed he will not break,
    and a faintly burning wick he will not quench;
    he will faithfully bring forth justice.
He will not grow faint or be discouraged
    till he has established justice in the earth;
    and the coastlands wait for his law. (Isaiah 42:1-4)

In those days and at that time I will cause a righteous Branch to spring up for David, and he shall execute justice and righteousness in the land. (Jeremiah 33:15)

God's throne is one of justice. A throne is the symbol of power and authority. It represents the place where kings rule, where decisions are made and where laws are enforced. Justice and righteousness are the foundation of God's throne. His whole leadership and kingship flow from this foundation. It is from the place of justice that his kingdom is established.

Righteousness and justice are the foundation of your
    throne;
    steadfast love and faithfulness go before you.
    (Psalm 89:14)

The LORD reigns, let the earth rejoice;
    let the many coastlands be glad!
Clouds and thick darkness are all around him;

> righteousness and justice are the foundation of his
> throne. (Psalm 97:1-2)

GOD'S DELIGHT IN JUSTICE

God loves justice. God not only *rules* in justice, he also *loves* justice. It is the delight of his heart. And as people made in the image of God, we need to remember that our deep passion for justice is a small reflection of what burns inside God's heart.

> For the LORD loves justice;
>> he will not forsake his saints.
> They are preserved forever,
>> but the children of the wicked shall be cut off.
>> (Psalm 37:28)

> But let him who boasts boast in this, that he understands and knows me, that I am the LORD who practices steadfast love, justice, and righteousness in the earth. For in these things I delight, declares the LORD. (Jeremiah 9:24)

God blesses justice. Another way Scripture reveals how much God delights in justice is the way it speaks of the blessings that belong to those who do justice. Blessings await those who help the oppressed and the poor. God will deal well with the one who pursues justice.

Blessed are they who observe justice,
>   who do righteousness at all times! (Psalm 106:3)

It is well with the man who deals generously and lends;
>   who conducts his affairs with justice. (Psalm 112:5)

Blessed is he whose help is the God of Jacob,
>   whose hope is in the LORD his God,
who made heaven and earth,
>   the sea, and all that is in them,
who keeps faith forever;
>   who executes justice for the oppressed,
>   who gives food to the hungry.
The LORD sets the prisoners free. (Psalm 146:5-7)

When a leader rules with justice, blessings of light and life flow to the people.

The God of Israel has spoken;
>   the Rock of Israel has said to me:
When one rules justly over men,
>   ruling in the fear of God,
he dawns on them like the morning light,
>   like the sun shining forth on a cloudless morning,
>   like rain that makes grass to sprout from the earth.
>   (2 Samuel 23:3-4)

God in Scripture honors justice. David's rule as king over Israel is honored because he ruled with justice. Though he was not perfect, Scripture remembers him as a king who ruled and reigned in justice. He is honored throughout history for his acts of justice.

> So David reigned over all Israel. And David administered justice and equity to all his people. (2 Samuel 8:15)

GOD'S DESIRE TO SEEK JUSTICE

Justice is commanded to his people. The desire of God's heart is for his people to display his glory and his goodness upon the earth. One of the primary ways communities experience the blessings of safety, love and goodness is when justice rules the land. For this reason, God commands his people to do justice and to hold onto it with all their might. We need to understand that "justice is the work of community. It cannot be pursued alone. Justice is a manifestation of Christ's body working at its very best."[6] God's desire is for justice to be overflowing into society as an ever-flowing stream, beginning with his people.

> So you, by the help of your God, return,
>> hold fast to love and justice,
>> and wait continually for your God. (Hosea 12:6)

> Hate evil, and love good,
>> and establish justice in the gate;
> it may be that the LORD, the God of hosts,
>> will be gracious to the remnant of Joseph. (Amos 5:15)

He has told you, O man, what is good;
> and what does the LORD require of you
but to do justice, and to love kindness,
> and to walk humbly with your God? (Micah 6:8)

So we see throughout Scripture that justice is heavy on God's heart. We were meant to treat one another with the righteous character of God. It is right and righteous living in the context of community. It is an expression of loving our neighbor as ourselves.

Now we will draw our attention to God himself, who is a God of justice. In this world that seems dominated with injustice and evil, what does a just God do? How does God establish justice in an unjust world? That will be the focus of the next chapter.

GROUP DISCUSSION QUESTIONS

- Which verses stood out to you the most, and why? Did anything surprise you about what Scripture says about justice or how often Scripture speaks of it?

- Who would be considered a vulnerable group in your community? Make a list of all the different types of vulnerable people in your area.

- Looking at the list, how many are being cared for by churches in your community? Is there something your church could do to love them?

PRAYER GUIDE

- Ask God to open your eyes to see the vulnerable people in your community with his eyes of love and compassion.

- Pray for the vulnerable in your community. Pray that they will be protected and cared for and know the love of Jesus.

- Pray for your church and the churches in your community to be active in sharing the love of Jesus in tangible ways to those who are in need.

WHERE IS THE
JUSTICE OF GOD?

The Lord works righteousness
and justice for all who are oppressed.

Psalm 103:6

Approximately 80% of trafficking victims are female,
50% are children, 70% for sexual exploitation.

US State Department

Injustice occurs when power is misused to take from others
what God has given them, namely, their life, dignity,
liberty or the fruits of their love and labor.

Gary Haugen

THE PROBLEM IS INJUSTICE IN THE WORLD

It only takes one look at the evening news to see there is something very wrong in this world. A drunk driver crashes into another car and walks away, while the driver in the other car will never walk again. The CEO of a large company is found guilty of stealing millions and faces a three-month probationary term, while a homeless man steals $100 and is sentenced to over fifteen years in jail. A fourteen-year-old girl is forced into a car, but the police officer nearby does nothing except count the money he just received from the trafficker and put the money into his shirt pocket, right behind his police badge. But one of the greatest injustices happening in our own backyard is the buying and selling of precious women and girls for exploitation within the global sex trade.

In response to injustices like these, our church members do prayer walks where women are sex trafficked within our city. They handed out flowers once on White Day, a Korean variation of Valentine's Day, to the female prostitutes and chocolate to the pimps as part of an outreach to the notorious Yongjugol red-light district near Seoul. Jacob Bennett, one of our team members, noticed the nearby police eying them suspiciously. Of course, seeing foreigners handing out flowers and candy is strange, but the police weren't at all suspicious of the pimps blatantly breaking the laws of Korea. They turned a blind eye to the soliciting going on right before them. The irony was tragic and sobering. One member said in disbelief, "The police were watching *us*. It never ceases to shock me and make me feel helpless." Later, when the team went to visit the head pimp of the area, they were invited into the basement for tea and coffee. "The head pimp even gave us a speech of thanks for loving on these girls who he thinks he is helping. I remember feeling sick."

There is great injustice in our world, but why? Why is there such evil surrounding us? There are many factors we can look at, but the Bible tells us the fundamental cause. We live in a fallen, sin-stained and broken world. Injustice occurs because there is great unrighteousness within the human heart. The apostle Paul tells us that "none is righteous, no, not one" (Romans 3:10) and "all have sinned and fall short of the glory of God" (Romans 3:23). The ultimate source of injustice is the sin that lies within the heart of every person on this planet. The apostle Paul tells Timothy that things will get even worse in the last days:

> But understand this, that in the last days there will come times of difficulty. For people will be lovers of self, lovers of money, proud, arrogant, abusive, disobedient to their parents, ungrateful, unholy, heartless, unappeasable, slanderous, without self-control, brutal, not loving good, treacherous, reckless, swollen with conceit, lovers of pleasure rather than lovers of God. . . . Indeed, all who desire to live a godly life in Christ Jesus will be persecuted, while evil people and impostors will go on *from bad to worse*, deceiving and being deceived. (2 Timothy 3:1-4,12-13, emphasis added)

The nature of sin is such that, if it is not dealt with properly, it grows. This is bad news.

Time and time again we see our world filled with brokenness and injustice. We can relate to the psalmist who becomes envious of the arrogant when he sees the wicked prosper (Psalm 73:3). It is frustrating and infuriating to see those who do evil get away with it. Because "there can be no peace without justice,"[1] there will be a restlessness in society until justice rules. During the 2008 financial crisis in the US, there were CEOs who walked away with million-dollar bonuses while millions of workers lost their jobs. That is a great injustice! Is there no one who notices? Is there no one who cares? Is there no one who can do something about these great injustices?

The answer to these cries is a resounding YES! YES! There is someone who notices! YES! There is someone who cares! And YES! There is someone who will do something about it!

Then what is the solution to this great problem of injustice in our world?

THE SOLUTION IS OUR GOD OF JUSTICE

God is the answer to the problem of injustice because God is the ultimate source of justice. "Therefore the LORD waits to be gracious to you, and therefore he exalts himself to show mercy to you. For the LORD is a God of justice; blessed are all those who wait for him" (Isaiah 30:18). This is a rich verse that exalts the grace and mercy of God in connection with the justice of God. God's solution to the injustice of man's rebellion is found in the grace of Jesus Christ that attained justice for all who would believe in him through his death upon the cross. "Many seek the face of a ruler, but it is from the LORD that a man gets justice" (Proverbs 29:26). Justice may come through an earthly judge or a court system, but according to Scripture the ultimate source of justice is God because he is the judge over all the earth.

This is good news, but what does it mean? J. I. Packer reminds us of the significance of God's role as judge.[2] Remember that a judge is a person identified with what is good and right. To be a judge means this person has moral excellence to make the right decision. He is not biased or impartial. Another attribute of a judge is great wisdom and the ability to discern truth. Also, a judge is someone who has power and authority to execute the sentence. He is able to do something about the wrong that has been committed. That is our God! So we do not worry or grow weary, because our God is the good judge over all the earth.

But if he is the judge and is able to do something, why does injustice still exist? Does he not care? He does care. He has done something about it. He will do something about it. And he desires the church to do something about it. Now it's important for us to look at the ways in which God brings about justice into the world.

GOD'S SOLUTION FROM THE BEGINNING—THE CROSS
When we see injustice in this world, we need to see it through

the lens of God's complete story of redemptive history. The scope of all of Scripture and the story that God is writing can be seen in these four movements: creation, fall, redemption, consummation. Ever since the fall (when sin and injustice entered our world), God had a plan, and that plan would be realized in the life, death and resurrection of his Son, Jesus Christ. Therefore Jesus is central to understanding where the justice of God can be found.

Let's begin by looking at what Jesus said at the start of his public ministry. Luke 4:16-19 says:

> And he came to Nazareth, where he had been brought up. And as was his custom, he went to the synagogue on the Sabbath day, and he stood up to read. And the scroll of the prophet Isaiah was given to him. He unrolled the scroll and found the place where it was written,

> "The Spirit of the Lord is upon me,
>   because he has anointed me
>   to proclaim good news to the poor.
> He has sent me to proclaim liberty to the captives
>   and recovering of sight to the blind,
>   to set at liberty those who are oppressed,
> to proclaim the year of the Lord's favor."

The ministry of Jesus was centered on justice. He came to declare good news to those who experienced bad news in this fallen world. Jesus came to right the wrongs done to the vulnerable and the oppressed. What does this justice look like? A quick read of these verses makes it sound like Jesus is only concerned with bringing about physical justice, but looking through the filter of his whole ministry reveals that he is concerned with both the physical and the spiritual condition of people.

People will quote these verses, especially the part of proclaiming liberty to the captives and setting the oppressed free, as the basis for fighting human trafficking. But we must keep in mind that there is both a physical and a spiritual element to justice. In the justice movement of our day, we *are* called on to care for the physical needs of the poor, the hurting and the captives. That is justice. But we must not lose sight of the fact that the primary mission of Jesus was to bring spiritual freedom, spiritual healing and a spiritual blessing to all who were captives of sin. If someone is free physically but never experiences spiritual freedom from sin, then that person will still be bound to chains that can harm them throughout eternity. Let us love people by seeking their freedom physically, spiritually and eternally.

A weakness of the evangelical church in recent history is that it has been concerned only about the spiritual freedom of the soul, with no vital concern about the physical condition of others. Thankfully, we are seeing changes in this mentality in the justice movement in our generation. We must realize that to truly love a person means to love their whole being— physically, spiritually, emotionally and mentally. To be only concerned for the spiritual welfare of a person makes the person feel like they are a project to work on or win over instead of a person to love.

What I have found time and time again is that when we love people by caring for their physical needs, it opens their hearts to hear the gospel message for spiritual freedom as well. But we must never use caring for the physical needs of others as our foot in the door to try and evangelize them. Let us be a generation that will simply love our neighbors in whatever way we can, whenever we have the opportunity. We must live out the gospel, not just say it. The gospel must be declared *and* demonstrated. It must be lived out in love as well as spoken in truth.

Let us now look back at how this opening statement of Jesus is grounded in the spiritual freedom he came to bring. Pastor Tim Keller points out, in his sermon titled "Justice," an important omission that Jesus makes when he quotes Isaiah 61. He stops mid-sentence in verse 2 of the Isaiah passage. Here again is the passage Jesus quotes:

> The Spirit of the Lord is upon me,
>> because he has anointed me
>> to proclaim good news to the poor.
> He has sent me to proclaim liberty to the captives
>> and recovering of sight to the blind,
>> to set at liberty those who are oppressed,
> to proclaim the year of the Lord's favor.

And then Jesus stops right there! Look at what he leaves out: "and the day of vengeance of our God; to comfort all who mourn." Now why would he do that? Is he trying to soften up the mission and the message? Hardly. The reason why Jesus leaves out the wrath of God at the start of his public ministry is because *he* is the one who will bear the wrath of God at the end of his public ministry. Jesus is saying, "I will not declare God's vengeance and wrath to you. Instead I will take God's vengeance and wrath *for* you!"

The good news is that Jesus is the one who will absorb the wrath and vengeance of God on the cross. John 3:16-17 tells us,

> For God so loved the world, that he gave his only Son, that whoever believes in him should not perish but have eternal life. For God did not send his Son into the world to condemn the world, but in order that the world might be saved through him.

Jesus came to take the vengeance, condemnation and wrath of God that was intended for us! My injustice against a holy, just God was dealt with when Jesus took my penalty. God had a plan to deal with sin, evil and injustice from the beginning, and the ultimate way he sought to deal with it was through the cross of Jesus Christ. John Stott says,

> By bearing himself in Christ the fearful penalty of our sins, God not only propitiated his wrath, ransomed us

from slavery, justified us in his sight and reconciled us to himself, but thereby also defended and demonstrated his own justice.[3]

Jesus' ministry was centered on fighting injustice. But before we start looking at the injustices of others, we need to begin by looking at the injustice in our own hearts. We begin by remembering that one of the greatest injustices of all is sinning and rebelling against a holy God. There is a penalty that must be enforced and a price that must be paid because of this great offense. We were supposed to receive that penalty, but Jesus took it for us. Jesus paid the price. He bore our punishment. He bailed us out. And Jesus bestowed on us his righteousness as he places us in him. This all happened when Jesus died on the cross for the sins of the world. God's solution for justice from the start was the cross of Jesus Christ. It is here that God rectified the great injustice of our rebellion through the death and resurrection of his only Son.

The great injustice of dishonoring God ends with the great justice of God receiving the worship due his name—for all who would put their trust in his name. This is the spiritual justice that changes lives for eternity and brings forth true freedom. It is the great act of grace that restores ultimate justice in the story of redemption.

All evil, injustice and wrongs have been dealt with for those who trust in Jesus Christ. But what about those who will not place their faith and trust in Jesus Christ? Where is the justice

for them? This leads us to another place where we find the
justice of God.

GOD'S SOLUTION AT THE END—THE JUDGMENT

The psalmist in Psalm 73 wrestles with the question of injustice and seeing the wicked prosper, but he is comforted
when he enters the "sanctuary of God" where he then understands their final destiny. For every evil, there will be a day of
justice. For every wrong done, for every injustice, there will
be a reckoning to face. It will be a day that will give each
person what they truly deserve. Jesus speaks of this end-time
judgment in John 5:22-29:

> The Father judges no one, but has given all judgment to
> the Son, that all may honor the Son, just as they honor
> the Father. Whoever does not honor the Son does not
> honor the Father who sent him. Truly, truly, I say to you,
> whoever hears my word and believes him who sent me
> has eternal life. He does not come into judgment, but
> has passed from death to life.
>
> Truly, truly, I say to you, an hour is coming, and is
> now here, when the dead will hear the voice of the Son
> of God, and those who hear will live. For as the Father
> has life in himself, so he has granted the Son also to have
> life in himself. And he has given him authority to ex-
> ecute judgment, because he is the Son of Man. Do not
> marvel at this, for an hour is coming when all who are

in the tombs will hear his voice and come out, those who have done good to the resurrection of life, and those who have done evil to the resurrection of judgment.

The Gospels make it clear that those who have not believed in the Son of God or trusted in Christ Jesus to save them from their sins will face a day of great judgment. But those who do trust in Christ as the only way to be saved from sins will experience a day of resurrection unto life!

We see this in Revelation 20:13-15:

And the sea gave up the dead who were in it, Death and Hades gave up the dead who were in them, and they were judged, each one of them, according to what they had done. Then Death and Hades were thrown into the lake of fire. This is the second death, the lake of fire. And if anyone's name was not found written in the book of life, he was thrown into the lake of fire.

Every person who has not surrendered their lives and sins to Jesus will face eternal judgment and damnation in the lake of fire forever. Every pimp who has profited from the sexual abuse of his captors, every trafficker who has destroyed the innocence of his victims, every customer who has stolen (not bought!) the sacred touch of intimacy from his victim, every person who has caused injustice to the least of these will face the full fury of God's wrath that has been stored up for generations! This wrath is saved up for all who have rejected the saving grace of Jesus Christ who came to forgive us from all of our sins. This wrath will bring forth justice for all of eternity.

Does God care? Oh, he cares! He weeps with his daughters who weep behind closed doors. He is angry at the treatment of his little girls, and he *will* demand justice to be served one day! That is why we cry out: *Maranatha,* "O Lord, come!" That is the cry of God's people who face injustice all the day long. This is why we pray for his return—in order to see justice fully established on the earth. On the final judgment day, all evil, injustice and sin will be dealt with. God will right all wrongs. Every sinner will get their just punishment. Every trafficker and pimp and John will get their due.

And we need faith in our God of justice to believe that he will deal with all the right way and in the right time. In the mighty chapter of faith in Hebrews 11, faith was required and honored in the establishing of justice—"who through faith conquered kingdoms, *enforced justice*, obtained promises, stopped the mouths of lions" (Hebrews 11:33, emphasis added). I never noticed that justice was in this chapter before, but the connection is clear—it takes faith to pursue justice. It takes faith to believe that our God is committed to justice in *all* the nations of the earth. It takes faith to believe that his purposes will prevail in the end. And it takes faith to *enforce* justice when it seems the world is against you. As the great hymn "This Is My Father's World" reminds us, "though the wrong seems oft so strong, God is the ruler yet!" So, does this mean we just wait and see who will trust God and who won't? Is the cross and the last judgment the only place and time we find God's justice? No. There is more.

God expects us to partner with him in establishing justice. What, then, is the role of the church today? And what is the connection between the cross, final judgment and today's actions for justice? Do we do nothing because all will work out in the end?

GOD'S SOLUTION FOR TODAY: THE CHURCH

Our justice movement must flow from these two realities of God's justice: the cross and the final judgment. If it does not keep one eye on the cross and one eye on eternal judgment in the end, then our movement will become a humanistic, self-righteous act rather than a biblical, gospel-centered one. If I don't look at the cross, I will think that the sins of the traffickers are worse than my own sins, and I can become arrogant, judgmental and self-righteous. The danger is to think that I am somehow better than they are and that I am the solution to the world's problems. If I don't look at the final judgment, I will become frustrated seeing all this evil around me. I will think that God is not fair or just.

Again, there are three places where we find God's justice: the cross, the judgment and the church. God's justice was initiated with the cross and it will be completed on judgment day. But justice must be sought out, expressed and established in faith and in love today. There is an *already/not yet* tension in which we are living concerning the coming of God's kingdom and the kingdom that is here.

> Although the kingdom is here in the finished work of Christ, the ministry of the Holy Spirit, and the witness of the church, this presence is partial and mysterious, for the kingdom is yet to be consummated. There remains a future eschatological aspect to the kingdom. Biblical theologians often say that the kingdom has been inaugurated, but is yet to be consummated, or that the kingdom is both already and not yet.[4]

The part of God's kingdom that is already here through the church must advance and show what the kingdom of God looks like as we walk in faith, hope and love.

But before we even think about dealing with the injustices of others, we need to deal with the injustice that we have done before God. Our first response toward injustice is to look to God in faith. It begins with faith in Christ for the forgiveness of my sins and the evils that I have committed throughout my life. Yes, there are great evils within this world that we must fight, but before I look at the speck of sawdust in my brother's eye, Jesus tells me to first take the log out of my own eye. If I honestly examine my heart, I will find that great evil lives within me as well. I need to kill it and surrender it at the feet of Jesus. I am a sinner who has committed great injustices, and I can only be freed and restored through faith in Christ.

Second, my response to those who do injustice is to pray they will put their hope in God. First Timothy 6:10 tells us that "the love of money is a root of all kinds of evils." That pretty much sums up the motive of trafficking at its core— greed. So after writing about how the love of money is a root of all kinds of evils, Paul then encourages Timothy to tell the churches "not to be haughty, nor to set their hopes on the uncertainty of riches, but on God, who richly provides us with everything to enjoy" (1 Timothy 6:17).

We preach the gospel so that all who are spiritually en-slaved will experience the freedom that Christ came to give. We must pray that every trafficker and pimp would be set free from the bondage of greed, lust and immorality and instead put their hope in Christ. Our desire is for society to bring them to justice, yes, but we also pray that they would be healed and restored from the things that bind them. As we keep our eyes on the cross and on the day of judgment, we seek to bring these people into a saving knowledge of Jesus so that their lives can be transformed by the gospel.

A third response for the church is to love the victims of injustice. The justice movement must be driven by love— for God and for our neighbor. Therefore we must feed the poor, clothe the naked and fight for the trafficked victim. Love, mercy, generosity—that is justice to God. You see, justice in God's kingdom is not just about upholding the law but about caring for the vulnerable and the broken in our communities. So the justice movement is one of the greatest ways to show love to our neighbors.

We are to love both the victims *and* the perpetrators. God will call some to focus their ministry efforts on those who have been trafficked, but God will call others to serve those who do the trafficking. Both require supernatural, unconditional love. We will look at examples of how some churches are doing this in chapter five of this book.

After Jesus says that loving God and loving our neighbors is the mark of true life, a lawyer asks Jesus "Who is my neighbor?" What he meant was, "Who don't I have to love?" In response, Jesus tells the parable of the good Samaritan and ends with this in Luke 10:36-37: "'Which of these three, do you think, proved to be a neighbor to the man who fell among the robbers?' He said, 'The one who showed him mercy.' And Jesus said to him, 'You go, and do likewise.'"

So who is the one who lived a life of proper love and justice? The one who showed mercy, love and generosity to those in need.

As it says in the book of Micah,

He has shown you, O mortal, what is good.
    And what does the Lord require of you?
To act justly and to love mercy
    and to walk humbly with your God. (Micah 6:8 NIV)

Where is justice? The world is meant to see it . . . in you!

GROUP DISCUSSION QUESTIONS

- Why is it important to begin our justice movement by looking to the cross of Jesus? Why should we examine our own injustice toward God first?

- How do you feel about the final day of judgment? Will it be a day of hope or horror? Explain.

- What is your current understanding of the church's role in seeking justice in this world?

PRAYER GUIDE

- Thank God for the ways the cross of Jesus has dealt with all the injustices of our sin.

- Pray for a deeper faith that trusts God to deal with all injustices in due time.

- Pray that your church will do its part in partnering with God and his gospel to bring forth justice in our generation.

EXPOSING THE DARKNESS OF MODERN-DAY SLAVERY

*"Cursed be anyone who perverts the justice due to
the sojourner, the fatherless, and the widow."
And all the people shall say, "Amen!"*

Deuteronomy 27:19

*Human trafficking affects every country
around the world, generating more
than $32 billion worldwide.*

Polaris Project

*Injustice anywhere is a threat
to justice everywhere.*

Martin Luther King Jr.

"Mindy" was the youngest daughter of a large family in a rural village in Thailand. As is common with many young girls raised in the Thai countryside, she grew up knowing she had to support her parents. So she took on the responsibility of being the main breadwinner for her family. She looked for a job in her village, but was unsuccessful because everyone struggled with poverty.

Then, one day, her uncle said he knew of a friend who could provide a job for her in the United States. Mindy had never traveled outside of her village before, but she decided make the sacrifice for the sake of her family. With her uncle's help, she got her first passport. When she received it, she became excited. Maybe she would be able to make money for the family after all. A friend of her uncle escorted her all the way from Thailand to Los Angeles International Airport. Upon arrival in the US, she was handed over to her new boss who owned the restaurant she would be working at.

At first, she began work as a waitress. Mindy was nervous because she didn't speak English and the work was hard. Then her boss asked for her passport. "Just to keep things safe," he said. Mindy decided to trust him. She handed over her passport.

The very next day, her boss told her, "You no longer work at the restaurant." He threw a new set of clothes at her and demanded she wear them. Mindy couldn't believe her eyes. The clothes were skimpy and promiscuous. As a shy girl from the country, she would never wear such clothes. When she refused, he hit her. Out of fear, she put on the clothes. Then he violated her and beat her some more. Bruised and in shock, Mindy was filled with shame.

From the next day onward, she had a new job of hosting men who would violate her every night. Though she ended up living in the US for two years, she only knew the inside of hotel rooms. Every three days, she would be taken to a new city and a new hotel room. With nowhere to run and no ability to communicate in this new land, she was utterly under the control of her boss.

I wish this story was rare, but it is not. This story is not just happening in LA, but in other cities like San Francisco and Shanghai and Seoul. This is the reality of human trafficking today. Thankfully for Mindy, an undercover officer was able to bring her captor to justice. But sadly there are many more Mindy's enslaved, even in your own city.

These women have names. They have stories. They have families. But as you read or hear about these women in the press, the temptation is to view them as faceless and nameless.

But a key first step in this battle against darkness is education—to make ourselves aware and informed. It is to know our enemy.

This chapter seeks to expose evil by shining light into what seems like murky, chaotic darkness. I have to warn you—the sheer magnitude of the statistics and facts may overwhelm you. Satan would prefer that we remain blind to this overview of modern-day slavery, that we leave this information hidden and unknown. Girls like Mindy and countless other women and children will then remain forgotten, their names and lives cloaked in darkness, hidden from the world in sordid hotel rooms, brothels and karaoke bars, never seeing the light of day.

Providing an overview of the contours of the problem means we boldly shed light into the darkness, revealing evil for what it really is and casting it out in Jesus' name—the name above all names.

In order to defeat evil, one of the first things we need to do is define the enemy. We need to assess their tactics, note their strength and troop movements, figure out their battle plans, identify their base camps (see Luke 14:28).

Let's assess the battlefield together.

THE BASICS

Let's start with some of the basics of human trafficking. There are three main types of trafficking happening in the world today:

- arms trafficking
- drug trafficking
- human trafficking

Each of these is a multibillion dollar industry. Though arms trafficking is the largest at the moment, human trafficking is becoming the fastest growing form of illegal enterprise around the world. The selling of bodies is a form of modern-day slavery and one of the greatest evils that has re-emerged in our generation.

There are more than thirty million slaves in our world today[1] with well over 100,000 people enslaved in the United States alone.[2] Of these victims, 80 percent are female, 50 percent are minors, and 70 percent are trafficked for sexual exploitation.[3]

Human trafficking is happening on every continent of the world. The 2006 Trafficking in Persons (TIP) Report states that 12.3 million worldwide are forced into bonded labor, child labor and sexual servitude. In 2004, the US government reported that approximately 600,000 to 800,000 people were victims of trafficking worldwide. There are an estimated 400,000 people entering Europe illegally each year.[4] Even a small and isolated country such as Iceland, with a population of only 250,000, has had trafficking cases reported.[5]

Human trafficking is crudely economic. It has become the preferred choice of activity among organized crime groups these days because of how lucrative it is and because of the relative ease of transporting their "goods." It is much easier to bring a person across international borders than drugs or weapons, and for profitability, the sale of a human life seems almost endless. For example, if you sell one gram of drugs, you can only sell it once. But if you sell a person, you can sell that person over and over again.

DEFINITION OF TRAFFICKING

The United Nations Office on Drugs and Crime defines human trafficking as

> the recruitment, transportation, transfer, harboring or receipt of persons, by means of the threat or use of force or other forms of coercion, of abduction, of fraud, of deception, of the abuse of power or of a position of vulnerability or of the giving or receiving of payments or benefits to achieve the consent of a person having control over another person, for the purpose of exploitation. Exploitation shall include, at a minimum, the exploitation of the prostitution of others or other forms of sexual exploitation, forced labor or services, slavery or practices similar to slavery, servitude or the removal of organs.[6]

It can also involve:

- Smuggling—taking people across borders illegally
- Kidnapping—taking people against their will
- Coercion—forcing people through manipulation
- Rape
- Drugging
- Imprisonment
- Theft
- Forgery
- Threat

SOURCE, TRANSIT AND DESTINATION COUNTRIES

Almost every country in the world has a recorded case of human trafficking, but each country's involvement differs, whether as a source, transit or destination. A source country is where the victims come from, a destination country is where the victims end up and a transit country is where they travel through to get from source to destination. For example, South Korea is a major source country for sexual trafficking victims and a destination country for both sex and labor trafficking. It is also a transit country, bringing in people from all over Asia and Europe who end up in Japan, Australia and the United States.

WHY PEOPLE ARE TRAFFICKED

These are the main arenas in which human trafficking occurs.

Labor exploitation. Labor exploitation is when people are trafficked to do manual labor within a given industry.[7] There are three main types of labor exploitation: sweatshops, housemaids and child labor.

The *sweatshop factory* setting requires people to work long hours with little or no pay. They are usually in an unsafe or unhealthy work environment, and it is not uncommon for these people to sleep, work and live in the same cramped and overcrowded room with many others. Though the term "sweatshop factory" implies an indoor workplace, the type of labor required can also be outdoor work, such as farming, brick making and other forms of slave labor. Another common factor is that they cannot leave their workplace on their own volition.

A common, though less recognized, form of labor exploitation is to work as a *housemaid*. This one is difficult to see or find because they are within a home setting they cannot leave. It may appear that the household has just a regular maid, but she is not free to come and go as she pleases.

Child labor is another growing problem in the world of human trafficking, forcing children to work long, hard hours, usually without pay. These children are taken away from their families and not allowed to attend school or play with their friends. They too are placed in unhealthy or dangerous work conditions. In some parts of Africa, children as young as eight are kidnapped and taken to cocoa farms to pick cocoa beans for fourteen to sixteen hours a day. Sadly, much of the chocolate and coffee that we consume on a daily basis is the fruit of their suffering. In Nepal, children are trafficked to weave carpets because of their small fingers, which are more effective in weaving together the very small and detailed designs that are popular. Instead of enjoying life as a child, they labor and suffer under slave conditions.

Marriages and mail-order brides. Many women around the world are sold into marriages, only to end up becoming slaves to their new "husbands" and families.[8] For example, because of China's one-child policy and preference for males, many baby girls have been aborted throughout the years. This has led to a massive imbalance between men and women, with men outnumbering the women. The resulting vacuum of Chinese women available for marriage to Chinese men has created a demand for women from abroad to become their wives. So, when North Korean refugees are caught crossing the border into China, the women are often tricked, trafficked or forced into these types of marriages.

It happens in other countries as well. Hmong refugees are often imported to the US as second wives for the Chinese men there.[9] In South Korea, the rural areas and farming communities are seeing a decrease of women available for these farmers to marry because most go to the big city in search of jobs. So mail-order brides are often "bought" from Southeast Asia (the Philippines, Vietnam, Cambodia, Thailand), but once they arrive, they are treated as property—slaves—and often beaten and abused by their new husbands.

Begging. Tragically, children are trafficked and forced to beg for money from wealthy tourists on the streets of cities around the world.[10] What these tourists don't realize is that these kids are beaten and not given food if they do not return with enough money for their owners. Others are mutilated in order to appear more helpless and gain sympathetic dollars from the visitors. In India, the "beggar mafia" will maim children on purpose to make them "better-looking beggars," often with the help of doctors who will do the maiming for the right price.[11] Kids are intentionally blinded, limbs are removed, and handicapped children are left without food and water so that a dehydrated appearance can add to the look of desperation.

Child soldiers. This is another very disturbing evil affecting children in different parts of the world. UNICEF estimates that over 300,000 children younger than eighteen are trafficked to serve in armed conflicts worldwide.[12] In Africa and Latin America, these child soldiers are ordered to fight in horrific wars. They are not only forced to bear arms, they are forced to kill their own family members in order to cut off any emotional ties to the world around them. After being traumatized by the violence, the young boys are trained to kill, rape and mutilate their victims, while girls are taken to be sex slaves for older men in the army.

Organ trafficking. This is a market driven by very rich, very sick people (in every sense of the word) who are in desperate need of organ transplants but cannot wait in line. The victims are often very poor men and women who did not intend to give up their organs. A host of problems arise with organ trafficking. The victims are usually forced to give up their organs even without any payment, and because of the illegal nature of this, the procedure is often done in poor sanitary conditions, resulting in serious health issues for the victims to deal with afterward, such as infections or even death. The World Health Organization (WHO) estimates that 10 percent of all 70,000 kidneys used for transplants each year are obtained on the black market.[13]

Adoption and orphans. Children are also trafficked for adoption from the developing world, primarily Latin America, Russia and Asia, to parents in North America and Western Europe who pay high fees to get these babies. In Southeast Asia, France, Greece and Bulgaria, pregnant women have been trafficked to secure their babies even from birth. "Orphan tourism" exists in Cambodia and other poor countries that promote "tourist specials" for visiting an orphanage. They take photos of these children and horrifically sexually exploit a child for a few dollars.[14]

Sexual exploitation. Sex trafficking is by far the most prevalent form of slavery today.[15] The victims are not just women either—men, women, boys and girls are all victims. It may take the common form of prostitution on the streets, but it can also disguised in the form of karaoke bars, massage parlors, nail salons and a host of other ways people pay to violate the bodies of these victims.

Indeed, several of our team members have reported being utterly shocked that the "respectable" neighborhoods in which they live here in Seoul have massage parlors and brothels tucked right around the corner. Elizabeth Lee was completely shocked to see that the hundreds of cards littering her neighborhood in Seoul as she came home from work and where children walked to school every day weren't advertisements for the local hair salon. These were openly advertising prostitution.

One day, after Elizabeth and our team prayed outside of a red-light district, she saw a taxi cab pull up. She told me, "A middle-aged Korean man stepped out. He went inside the alley to one of the brothels closest to the street. He walked in and then a few minutes later, he returned to the cab with a big envelope of money. Inside the taxi cab, his elementary school-aged son was waiting. And that was when I realized the depth of depravity that existed here. I saw how the sex industry wasn't just isolated to madams, pimps, women or johns. Rather, I saw that it affected families. My heart sank as I thought about the younger generation and what they would be growing up into."

WHO ARE THE VICTIMS?

Women. Women and girls are the most trafficked group in the world. They account for 80 percent of all human trafficking victims. "Trafficking most frequently occurs in societies where women lack property rights, cannot inherit land and do not enjoy equal protection under the law."[16] But it happens in nations where women have rights too. According to the US Attorney General report on trafficking in 2006, South Koreans accounted for the highest population (24%) of sex-trafficking victims in the US.[17] The popularity of Korean pop-culture around the world, with their girl bands dressed specifically to showcase their long legs as well as Korean dramas that are now more popular in Southeast Asia than Hollywood movies, has created a high demand for Korean women in brothels all around the world.

This reveals the complex nature of global sex trafficking. It's often assumed that the victims of sex trafficking come from the poorest countries, but as we can see, South Korea—which has roughly the same per capita GDP as Italy and is considered a wealthy and developed country—is a major source country for sex trafficking. Clearly, there are complex

"push and pull" factors that crisscross international bound-
aries. In Japan, another affluent and developed nation, there
is the tragic phenomenon of *enjo kosai*, where young Japanese
teenagers date older men, often exchanging sex for money to
buy luxury items such as designer purses. For many South
Korean women, debt bondage is also a major factor in
"pushing" women to seek money overseas. Incurring large
amounts of debt, they travel overseas only to find that they
are preyed upon by immoral brokers who only add on to their
already huge debt. With their passports and status taken from
them, many become trapped in the cycle of human trafficking.
Some have tried to argue that many of these Korean women
would not classify as victims of trafficking because they
"voluntarily" left their country, lured by the prospect of a job
by shady brokers. Once abroad, however, they cannot leave.

Children. Many children in third-world countries are particularly susceptible to traffickers who use them for labor and
sexual exploitation.[18] Though child prostitution is illegal all
over the world, estimates say there are over two million
children who are forced into the global sex trade. Many men,
for fear of HIV and diseases in older women, prefer having sex
with children since they are less likely to carry disease. Vir-
ginity is highly valued in some cultures, with men willing pay
high sums of money for a child who is still a virgin. In fact, in
some cultures, people think that having sex with a virgin will
cure them of certain diseases like AIDS, creating a higher
demand for younger and younger children. Not only does the

child become infected with diseases, some end up addicted to drugs that the trafficker supplies to them. Others get pregnant and most are malnourished. If intervention does not happen soon, they face an early death.

Men. Men are also trafficked, but primarily for forced manual labor or to work on fishing boats. Due to debt that the man must pay off, or threats to the safety of his family, the victim has little choice but to live as a slave until someone can help set him free. In India, some men are paying off past generations of debt that began with their father or even grandfather. The cycle often continues as children who are born during this time of slavery will inherit the debt incurred by the parents. From an early age, they are raised into thinking that slavery is their identity.[19]

The stateless. The TIP Report 2009 estimated that twelve million people are stateless around the world. Stateless people have no legal proof of citizenship, so they are unable to register a birth, educate their children, get health care, work or even travel legally. They have no protection from police or government or legal systems, which leaves them incredibly vulnerable to traffickers.[20] They are one of the most vulnerable groups in the world. Many stateless people can be found among the hill tribes of northern Thailand, the Roma in Europe and the Haitian migrants in the Caribbean.

A growing number of stateless children emerged recently in South Korea. Migrant workers from Southeast Asia have children with US military men, but the men leave the country and leave undocumented children in their wake. Without the support of their father, neither the US nor South Korea nor even the mother's home country will give the child citizenship. Thus, thousands of children are left stateless and vulnerable.

Some surveys have estimated that of all the women working the red-light districts in Thailand, over 80 percent of them are stateless females from a northeast region called Isaan. Because they are stateless, the only working visa the Thai government gives them is for the sex industry. If that is the case, is it really a choice? One small ray of light is that the Thai government will give citizenship to the stateless if they graduate with a university degree. This opens up a whole new world of opportunities for them. Upon learning about this, our church has created scholarships to help stateless children in Thailand attend university, so that finances will never be a reason for not finishing.

In a similar way, refugees are left vulnerable to a government that will not provide safety and shelter for them. The dangerous plight of North Korean refugees who cross over from their nightmare in North Korea into China is that they will not always have a better life waiting for them. Many North Korean refugees in China end up being sold as unwilling brides or are sex trafficked throughout the world.

The poor. Those who are poor or paying off large amounts of debt become vulnerable to the world of sex trafficking. Those who need large sums of money will fall prey to loan sharks who charge astronomical amounts of interest that the debtors are unable to pay.[21] Many women who end up in the sex industry in South Korea are victims of this type of debt bondage. Sometimes, through credit card debt or high medical bills due to sudden health crises within their family, they need large amounts of money in a short amount of time. They are unable to get a legitimate loan through the bank, so they turn to loan sharks who enslave them in the sex industry to pay off their debts.

The orphan. In Moldova and other parts of Europe, there are known cases where even orphanage staff partner with traffickers to tell them when girls will "age out" of the orphanage and hook them up with "lover boys" who will pose as interested boyfriends, only to sell them to traffickers once they buy into the lie of the boyfriend's love for her. Sadly, because no one has adopted or cares for them, many will disappear once they leave the system. With no family, no one knows when they go missing.

CAUSES

Depending on who you talk to, there are various reasons for the spread of human trafficking around the world. From a political and economic standpoint, some will say *globalization,* or the growing disparity between the rich and poor, is the cause.

> The supply exists because globalization has caused increasing economic and demographic disparities between the developing and developed world, along with the

feminization of poverty and the marginalization of many
rural communities.[22]

Along those lines, the lack of employment opportunities
and increasing poverty is the reason this exists. From a sociological perspective, a low view of women and children is seen
as the cause. "Women and female children are particularly
vulnerable to trafficking because of their low social status and
the lack of investment in girls."[23]

Yet, digging deeper, there is another common cause for all
the trafficking happening around the world: corruption.
Sometimes local law enforcement is paid to look the other
way, in other cases it's the immigration officers. Whatever the
case, corruption is often endemic in the justice systems that
allow this injustice to run rampant.

But more than a product of political, economic or even
sociological factors, we must see human trafficking for what
it truly is: a great moral evil that has corrupted the heart. It
is a spiritual issue at its core, which is why the church must
be involved. If we boil it down to its lowest common de-
nominator, we will see that greed and lust are the driving
forces for this evil. It is the love of money that is a root of all
kinds of evil, and we see the seed of greed sprout the weeds
of wickedness all around us. Profits from sex exploitation
alone each year generates over $33.9 billion![24]

In light of such evil, what can be done? Our efforts seem
so puny in the face of such staggering sums.

In February 2013, we invited Don Brewster and his wife, Bridget, the founders of Agape International Missions (AIM), to speak at our Justice Conference. The couple moved to Cambodia in 2006 and later founded Rahab House, which provides outreach, education and aid for sex trafficking victims.

In the face of the enormity of evil, Don reminded us that Jesus is the one who leaves the ninety-nine to go after the one.

He told us the story of what he calls "the one"—a tough Cambodian girl named Srey Leak. Srey Leak was born in 1996, but she's seen more horror than most adults ever will. She came to Rahab House at a time when they simply didn't have the money or resources to take on one more person. To do so would have put the other girls under the Brewsters' care in jeopardy. As for Srey Leak, she wasn't interested in any kind of shelter. She was broke and without food. How could Rahab House possibly help her?

Like many others, Srey Leak came from a broken family. Her father was an alcoholic who regularly beat her. Srey Leak ran away from home and found herself alone on the streets of Phnom Penh. Like so many young girls, she ended up in the sex trade where she underwent horrific abuse and torture. She lost her innocence at the hands of cruel men who exploited her young teenaged body for sheer profit. She bounced from one karaoke bar to another before ending up in the notorious Svay Pak area.

You might wonder why Srey Leak didn't go back home. But in Cambodia, there is a saying: *Boys are like gold and girls are like cloth.* Once soiled, cloth is good for nothing and girls become dirty rags. Srey Leak really believed this. She felt that she had no other choice in life but to work in karaoke bars.

But in following Jesus, Don decided to focus on the one—this special girl, despite the lack of money.

The Brewsters took her in. What a difference! While the greedy brothel kicked Srey Leak out because she had gotten pregnant twice (she was forced to abort both babies) and was producing no money for them, the Brewsters took her in even though they had no money for the next month!

When Srey Leak first came to Rahab House, she had no intention of staying. She resisted every step of the way. But the staff doctor examined Srey Leak's incredibly damaged body and told her she needed proper medication and rest. She reluctantly agreed to spend the night.

That first night for Srey Leak was long. Lights out at Rahab House is nine o'clock, but Srey Leak's night usually started then and didn't end till five in the morning. The other girls were so nice to her and Srey Leak was amazed by their kindness. Srey Leak thought this was "cool." The next day, she was asked to help out with the kids' Bible camp. She hated kids, but to her surprise she discovered an emotion she hadn't felt in years—joy.

A few more weeks went by. The food was okay and the girls were nice, but Srey Leak had no interest in going to church or attending the morning Bible study the girls kept inviting her to. She preferred to sleep in.

But eventually, the love of Rahab House won her over. Don

and his staff continued to focus on this one girl, pouring out love to her in the littlest of ways. One day, she announced: "I want to learn more about Jesus . . . and I want to know more about those heavenly things."

Srey Leak started going to morning Bible study. Two weeks later, she accepted Christ. Two days after Christmas, she was baptized. Now she works with the other rescued girls in making bracelets and jewelry and even joined the worship team. She says, "I can make a good living and I have honor now."

For the first time in her life, Srey Leak had value and respect.

As Don Brewster said, "I wish that we could look inside her heart to see the *true* transition, to really be able to see inside someone's heart who thinks they are completely a worthless piece of trash. To be transformed and believe that God wants them, that God loves them, that he cherishes them so that they are driven to worship Christ and lead others to do it—it's a miracle."[25]

In light of such glory, words fail. Yes, our actions can make cataclysmic differences in the spiritual realms. I believe heaven rocked with joy as they celebrated Srey Leak's rescue. And darkness shuddered, cowered and fled at the power and light emanating from Srey Leak's transformed life.

As Srey Leak's story shows, the *driving force* behind sex trafficking is the lust of the flesh in the hearts of men and women around the world. Romans 1 reveals that hearts and minds grow darker the more we reject God and refuse to honor him as God. The fundamental cause of the evil of human trafficking is a spiritual cause. And Srey Leak's salvation also shows that this spiritual problem is in need of a spiritual solution, which is why the church must take the lead in this battle. That is what we will discuss in the next chapter.

GROUP DISCUSSION QUESTIONS

- Looking at the list of why people are trafficked, is there an area that gripped your heart more than others? Share.

- Are you interested in researching for yourself the presence of trafficked humans in your community? Looking at the list of who the victims of trafficking are, how many can be found within your own community?

- What do you believe is the primary cause of the growth of trafficking in our day?

PRAYER GUIDE

- Pray through the list of people who are most vulnerable to trafficking, and ask the Lord to protect them in your country and throughout the world.

- Pray for the children who are currently living in the nightmare of forced labor and sexual exploitation, and ask the Lord to heal them and set them free even today.

- Pray for God's light to reveal injustices in your community and for those evils to be driven away.

WHY THE CHURCH MUST LEAD

He has told you, O man, what is good;
and what does the LORD require of you
but to do justice, and to love kindness,
and to walk humbly with your God?

Micah 6:8

Every year, nearly 2 million children are exploited
in the global commercial sex trade.

UNICEF

Christ has no body on earth but yours,
no hands but yours, no feet but yours. Yours are the eyes
through which is to look out Christ's compassion to the world.
Yours are the feet with which he is to go about doing good.
Yours are the hands with which he is to bless men now.

Saint Teresa of Ávila

A BUMP IN THE ROAD

One day, a contact enabled me to meet a high-ranking official in the South Korean government to discuss the issue of human and sex trafficking in his nation. He had the authority and power to make decisions, and the word on the street was that he had the ears of the highest levels of state. I was grateful for the opportunity to meet with this very prestigious political figure. I figured that once he heard the shocking facts of this issue, he would be able to convey the information to the right people, and perhaps something might get done.

To my astonishment, he simply nodded his head and brushed past my presentation. Then, taking my arm and leading me aside, he spoke to me privately, as if this were "off the record."

"Why are you doing this?" he asked.

I was confused. Had he not just heard our discussion? Did we need a translator? I again went over the seriousness of human trafficking and its impact on the country.

"Yes, but why are you doing this? Don't you know that all men do this? Haven't you done this?"

I was astounded by his bluntness. He literally thought that human trafficking was not a serious problem. His message to me was, *You don't belong here. You shouldn't be doing this.*

Later, when I discovered the real estate blueprints of one of the most infamous red-light areas in Seoul, I learned that parts of the land on which it was situated were actually owned by the government and that they leased these properties to some of the largest pimps and organized criminal gangs. I shouldn't have been surprised. This is the way the world responds.

However, that was from a worldly government. True, I had hopes that this powerful official would listen to me, but then again, we are dealing with people and institutions that do not know God. What surprised me most was the reaction I got closer to home. I expected rejection and misunderstanding from the world, but I didn't expect a similar reaction from my own church and other Christians who began to hear of our work.

As I preached on biblical justice, I was so excited to see the changes that were happening in our church and the passion for God's justice that was growing within the hearts of our congregation members. But as word spread about how our church was trying to end human trafficking, I started getting some strong emails questioning our involvement in this movement.

"Are you turning into a social gospel church?"

"I'm worried about you, Eddie. I don't like what I'm hearing about the direction you're taking your ministry."

I even received an email from someone who said, "I have to admit I have never heard any of your sermons, but based on what I'm hearing about your church, I know you're a social gospel preacher." His message was clear. The church doesn't belong in these parts of society. In short, *You don't belong here.*

The emails, criticism and attacks surprised me.

From the moment I first found out about the evil of human trafficking, I knew in my heart that the church needed to be involved. I never doubted and never had to debate whether we as a church needed to begin this journey toward justice.

Though it made sense in my mind, I knew I needed to study Scripture further to make sure I could defend our involvement in this justice movement biblically. This was one motivating factor for writing this book. So if you as a pastor or church leader are reading this book in the hopes of beginning a justice ministry in your own church, then chances are you too will face some opposition. You may wonder if pursuing freedom and justice is biblical. I hope that the following chapters can help you see the heart of God through the lens of Scripture and grow a strong conviction that pursuing justice is a central part of God's heart for the world. A justice ministry will not look the same for every church, but I believe every church is called to pursue justice. It may be through prayer, it may be through preaching, or it may be through starting a full-blown ministry, but every church has a role to play in bringing an end to one of the greatest evils of our generation—modern-day slavery.

SOME COMMON OBJECTIONS

It's not the church's role to be involved. Let the "experts" handle it. Stick to the gospel. Stick to ministry!

It's just a passing fad. Stop chasing the latest "trend."

Isn't it too dangerous?

My responses to these are immediate: First, fighting for justice *is* an expression of the gospel. Didn't Jesus come to set the captives free? Don't these people who are trafficked and the traffickers need the visible and verbal presence of the church in their lives?

My response to those who ask, "Shouldn't you just stick to ministry?" This *is* ministry!

Second, this evil is so great, so systemic, so massive and entrenched that it's foolish to call it a passing fad or a trend. The slavery of today is worse than during the time of William Wilberforce, and look how long it took him to eradicate England's slave trade! This is no passing fad, and we should not have a sprinter's mentality. We need to be committed for the long haul. Anyone who thinks social justice is a passing fad is woefully blind to reality and historical figures like Wilberforce who had to battle such dismissive attitudes.

And finally, yes! It is dangerous! After all, we are dealing with organized crime and violent men. During one trip to Thailand, a few of our team members and I went to a nearby convenience store to buy some ice cream after a long day of ministry. While we were walking along a very deserted and dusty road back to our guesthouse, we saw down the road a man twisting the arm of a lady. She kept trying to grab the keys for her scooter out of this man's hand, but he wouldn't give them back to her. She was clearly in pain. We took a few steps closer and realized that she was dressed like the women in the red-light districts. The man was acting very much like her pimp. I wanted to help her, but I was also calculating the risks. What if he had a gun or a knife? He was already very upset, so I wouldn't want to upset him further. But as I was calculating our safety, Buri—our administrative staff who was also our team member on that trip—nudged me on the arm saying, "Pastor Eddie! Do something!" So I looked around and saw that we were able to outnumber him. Also, one of the guys with me named JJ was pretty big, so I decided to help the lady.

As we walked closer to him, I could feel my heart beating faster and faster. I quickly reviewed the self-defense classes I took when I was a boy in case something were to happen. But right before we reached them, I said to JJ, "You got my back, right JJ?" No answer. "JJ?" I looked around and all I saw was wide-eyed Buri silently clapping as I was about to confront this man. Further behind me, way across the street, was JJ who said he'd look after our other team members!

There was no time to turn around now. Here I was face to face with a man who was hurting and abusing a lady. So after taking a deep breath, I asked him, "Whose keys are those?" He stared long into my eyes and pointed his face toward the lady. With my heart pounding as if it were going to come out of my chest, I reached for the keys, took them out of his hand and gently gave them back to the lady, saying, "If these keys belong to her, we should give them back to her." He let go of her arm. I asked her if she was OK and she nodded her head saying she was. She thanked me and then quickly started the engine of her scooter and sped away. Thankfully, he also walked away and I rejoined the rest of our team. Buri was so happy, but I was still catching my breath and extremely thankful for my safety!

We must be as wise as serpents in this battle. But if this were your son or daughter being violated, wouldn't you want the world to know about it and do something? There may be risks involved, but their lives are worth it.

True faith always involves risk.

The church has gotten too used to not taking risks. For far too long we've let governments and NGOs do what God has called the church to do. We are letting others take the role of the church in our communities and forgetting that Jesus was the great abolitionist. In fact, we're letting the world take over our identity!

God calls the church to care for orphans, but we have left that to the agencies.

God calls us to feed the poor, but we have left that for our governments to take care of.

God calls us to defend the rights of the oppressed and to care for the vulnerable, but we have left that to the NGOs.

No, that is *our* job. It is what Jesus commanded.

Looking back, it is strange that I never once had to wonder if our church was supposed to be engaged in the fight to free those enslaved in our world today. I never thought, *Does the church belong here?* It was a natural overflow of seeing what was happening, praying and responding in obedience.

But that's an important question to ask: Does the church belong here? Does the church belong in this fight for the freedom of those enslaved by human traffickers? Are we in the right place? The answer is an emphatic *yes*!

And here's why.

THIS IS THE MISSION OF GOD

In this fight against the great evil of human trafficking in our day, it is my firm conviction that the church must not just be involved, it must lead the way in the pursuit of freedom and justice. Why do I say this? Because true freedom and justice can only come through the gospel of Jesus Christ. Freedom and justice are why Jesus Christ came to this earth. He came to bring forth ultimate freedom from sin and to establish ultimate justice through his death on the cross.

> But thanks be to God, that you who were once slaves of sin have become obedient from the heart to the standard of teaching to which you were committed, and, having been set free from sin, have become slaves of righteousness. (Romans 6:17-18)

The mission of Jesus was to die on the cross and be our atoning sacrifice so that we might be set free from sin. Sin is the problem that has affected all people. As we saw in the last chapter, the injustice of human trafficking is, at its core, a sin problem, not an economic problem.

I was traveling to speak at a conference in Asia when I

struck up a conversation with a person who was sitting next to me. She asked where I was headed, and I told her about the human trafficking conference I was attending. She was surprised that slavery still existed but suddenly paused and said, "I bet it's because of poverty that this happens. If people weren't poor, then this wouldn't happen." Her answer matched many others I've heard on this journey.

Does poverty alone really account for the existence of human trafficking? Even if being poor was the sole factor, Jesus has something to say to the poor:

> The Spirit of the Lord is upon me,
>> because he has anointed me
>> to proclaim good news to the poor.
> He has sent me to proclaim liberty to the captives
>> and recovering of sight to the blind,
>> to set at liberty those who are oppressed,
> to proclaim the year of the Lord's favor. (Luke 4:18-19)

The good news for the poor is that though you having nothing in this world, you can be rich in Christ. The good news for the poor is that wealth in this world is not the currency of true riches in heaven.

Consider the testimony of one young woman, still a teenager, who found that she had no choice but to sell her body because of money. The path to that nightmare life began not just with family dysfunction or poverty, but with evil.

She told us she was raped at the tender age of six, and then again at ages ten, twelve and fifteen. The shocking reality is that these acts were committed by members of her own family. Evil wished to stain her innocence forever with the shame. Without feeling any form of safety at home, she decided it was time to run away and take her chances on the streets. She was only fifteen at the time. Without any resources, she was noticed by a pimp and lured into the sex trade where she ended up sleeping with up to a dozen men each night.

She said, "I thought I had to do it because of money at first, but the more I did it, the more I felt dirty. I washed up after it was over and when I looked at myself in the mirror I felt really dirty. I scrubbed myself until my skin almost peeled off, but I still didn't feel clean."

Money alone wasn't what really drove her into the sex industry. The repeated childhood rapes that stole her innocence began the devastating path of brokenness. No amount of money can address the tremendous wounds that cut the little six-year-old girl to the core of her soul, even long after the physical wounds to her body were healed.

Other rescued woman we have interviewed told us they'd been beaten, some held at knifepoint, one almost choked to death. But what hurt them the most? One rescued woman told us very calmly in a quiet but firm voice: "Listening to someone telling me that I was a 'whore.' Things such as, 'You're nothing but a slut,' or 'I bought you. You belong to me and you're nothing but trash.'"

She paused. "That hurt me the most."

Another woman echoed this sentiment in our interview with her: "Sometimes I didn't feel like I was human. . . . We are not some object you can buy with money. I wish [the johns] would at least treat us as humans."

Evil strips us of our humanity, the perpetrator and the victim alike. Without true hope and healing for the brokenness and wounds that have been inflicted on these women, the wounds will remain. Which is why we are establishing the House of Hope in Korea. It will be the first Christ-centered, gospel-based aftercare center for victims of sex trafficking in Korea. We truly believe it is the gospel that ultimately will set these women free.

Thus, the deeper root of human slavery today is sin. And the reason Jesus came to this earth was to deal with the sin problem within every human heart. Jesus became the sacrificial lamb who would pay the penalty of our sins *and* set us free from the power of sin that controls our lives. A major part of God's mission is to set us free from the bondage of sin. Another way of saying this is that Jesus came to set the captives free! This is our message. This is our mission!

What are the real issues we are up against when it comes to human trafficking and modern-day slavery? It is a heart issue. It is a moral issue. It is a spiritual issue at its core.

- The lust of the johns
- The greed of the traffickers
- The self-hatred and shame of the victims

- The hopelessness of the imprisoned
- The suffering of all who are still on the road to recovery

Everyone is in bondage concerning this issue, and only Christ can set them free. Only Jesus can restore hope and bring forth new life. The church has the only message that can set them free, not just physically, but spiritually and for eternity. It is through declaring the gospel message that true freedom will be realized, for Jesus Christ is the great abolitionist.

Jesus says, "You are the light of the world" (Matthew 5:14), and "You are the salt of the earth" (Matthew 5:13), meaning you are change agents for society. Where there is darkness, you are to shine and provide warmth. You shine so that people can find the way, and provide warmth in the form of love to those who have lived in the cold of darkness for too long.

One day, members of our praise team visited Durebang ("My Sister's Place"), a shelter for migrant woman escaping sex trafficking in the nearby city of Pyeongtaek. One of the women there was a Catholic Filipina worker in her late twenties who wore dark sunglasses, even indoors. She told the praise team her story, recounting how she had been lured into a job here and then tricked into an establishment that served as a cover for prostitution. Like so many others, many women from Southeast Asia and elsewhere come to South Korea under entertainment visas, with promises to work in legitimate bars or restaurants, only to find themselves exploited and coerced into the sex trade.

When the members of the praise team handed out sheet music and led a mini praise set together, the woman enthusiastically followed along in English even though she wasn't familiar with any of the songs. Suddenly, in the midst of praising, she started to cry. The tears rolled down her face from behind her dark sunglasses. All her longing and pain from the past few months spilled out. She was just so happy to be able to praise God in the midst of all this. The praise team returned to Seoul deeply moved. This woman reminded them of what true praise is all about. We don't praise God because we have it all together. We praise him because we are in need and he meets us in our time of need.

There are few things darker in this world than the buying, selling and abuse of a human life. Light is needed in dark places, and this is where the church must go. This is the mission of God: to bring light, life and liberty into this world of darkness, death and bondage.

You see, the mission God gives us is to both *declare* the gospel and *demonstrate* the gospel through our lives. Of course, the primary and most important element of our mission is to declare the good news of the gospel that Jesus Christ alone can save us from our sin as we place our faith in him. So while evangelism to the lost must be primary, it is not the only thing we are called to do when being a gospel witness. Evangelism is priority, but meeting the physical needs of others in love is also needed so that they will not only hear about God's love, they will see in action too. James 2:17 tells us that if faith does not manifest in caring for the needs of others, then it is dead.

Jesus shows us how we humans should relate to each other. Jesus is the true embodiment of humanity. He is a picture of a human being fully alive. Through his life we see that defending the poor, the weak, the marginalized and the oppressed is a demonstration of the visible gospel. Jesus showed through *action* that there is a God who loves them. Likewise, our justice ministry is a practical way to love our neighbor as ourselves.

There was one fire station that had as its mission, "To save lives, property, and resources." And during 9/11, when lives needed saving, everyone ran away from the Twin Towers except the firefighters. Why? Their mission is to save lives, and sometimes fulfilling that mission requires them to head into dangerous situations. Our mission as the church is also to save lives. For some of us, it will also mean going to some difficult places. And if we're going to finish the mission Jesus gave us, it means going to places that are really dark and ugly because they are in desperate need of the gospel.

Not only is this the mission of God but also . . .

THIS IS THE VOICE OF GOD

I often hear people say how important it is to be a "voice for the voiceless" in this movement for freedom. I completely understand what they mean and where they are coming from, and I agree. Proverbs 31:8-9 even says, "Speak up for those who cannot speak for themselves, for the rights of all who are destitute. Speak

up and judge fairly; defend the rights of the poor and needy"
(NIV). Since the voice of the prisoner is not being heard, we must
echo their cries for help and their demands for justice.

But as believers, I believe our higher responsibility is not
just to be a voice for the voiceless. It is to be the voice of God
to the world. We are in this battle not just to answer the cry
of the victim, but to answer the cry of God's heart to see
justice roll down like a mighty river (Amos 5:24). Our voice
must represent the voice of God to the world!

God's voice declares:

> Learn to do good;
> seek justice,
>   correct oppression;
> bring justice to the fatherless,
>   plead the widow's cause. (Isaiah 1:17)

When we declare that a child growing in the womb is a life
made in the image of God, we are letting this nation hear the
voice of God. When we say, "Adoption is a beautiful thing!"
we are revealing God's heart for the orphan.

> God has taken his place in the divine council;
>   in the midst of the gods he holds judgment:
> "How long will you judge unjustly
>   and show partiality to the wicked?
> Give justice to the weak and the fatherless;
>   maintain the right of the afflicted and the destitute.

Rescue the weak and the needy;
>   deliver them from the hand of the wicked."
>   (Psalm 82:1-4)

God's voice must be heard! One of the roles our justice ministry has for the world and the churches is to declare God's voice and God's heart for the oppressed. You are salt, you are light, and you are to be change agents in society.

The church must also lead because . . .

THIS IS THE IMAGE OF GOD

Another key reason the church must lead is that the fight for justice shows the world what God looks like.

Blessed is he whose help is the God of Jacob,
>   whose hope is in the LORD his God,
who made heaven and earth,
>   the sea, and all that is in them,
who keeps faith forever;
>   who executes justice for the oppressed,
>   who gives food to the hungry.

The LORD sets the prisoners free;
>   the LORD opens the eyes of the blind.
The LORD lifts up those who are bowed down;
>   the LORD loves the righteous.
The LORD watches over the sojourners;
>   he upholds the widow and the fatherless,

> but the way of the wicked he brings to ruin. (Psalm
> 146:5-9)

This is a portrait of our God. So when we seek justice, show mercy, give generously and extend kindness, what we are doing is showing people what our God looks like.

> For the LORD your God is God of gods and Lord of lords,
> the great, the mighty, and the awesome God, who is not
> partial and takes no bribe. He executes justice for the
> fatherless and the widow, and loves the sojourner, giving
> him food and clothing. (Deuteronomy 10:17-18)

In his book *Generous Justice*, Tim Keller mentions how when he is a guest speaker somewhere, people will often ask him how he would like to be introduced. For that short introductory period he needs to select the primary things he wants to be known for. When I am introduced, I will sometimes not mention to people that I teach at Torch Trinity Graduate University or that I'm editor in chief of the devotional magazine *Living Life*, because my primary job is the lead pastor of Onnuri English Ministry in Seoul, South Korea. It's the main title on my business card.

What about God's business card? How would he be introduced as a guest speaker? One of the primary things that God does in this world is care for the poor and oppressed. The heart of God has always loved the poor, the orphan and the widow. Moreover, many of these people are shuttled between international borders. They are forced to migrate and are

stranded in strange lands against their will. They are the
modern sojourners of today—the very same weary, frightened
strangers whom God commanded us in Scripture to protect
and care for.

> The Lord works righteousness
> and justice for all who are oppressed. (Psalm 103:6)

> "Cursed be anyone who perverts the justice due to the
> sojourner, the fatherless, and the widow." And all the
> people shall say, "Amen." (Deuteronomy 27:19)

Who are the sojourners, the fatherless and the widows in
Scripture? They have always been the most vulnerable people
in society. God's heart has always been passionate about the
outcast and the oppressed. If they are vulnerable, then they
are valuable to the Lord. When I realized that they are the
MVPs, so to speak, here on earth, how I viewed the vulnerable in our community was totally transformed. Jesus
made it clear that caring for them is also caring for him (see
Matthew 25).

Doing the good work of God shows others the goodness of
God in us. As Kevin DeYoung writes, "We do good works to
show the world God's character and God's work."[1]

> Let your light shine before others, so that they may see
> your good works and give glory to your Father who is
> in heaven. (Matthew 5:16)

> You are the salt of the earth. (Matthew 5:13)

Jesus calls us the light of the world, and when he says that no one hides a lamp, it means you don't stay away from dark places. You shine into them.

Trafficking today is one of the darkest evils in existence. I believe part of the reason why it has become such an enormous problem is because the church has ignored and avoided it for far too long. It is time for that to change, beginning today. As people of light, we must find ways to shine the light of God and the love of God into these places.

The church must also lead because . . .

THIS IS THE MOVE OF GOD

> For everything there is a season, and a time for every matter under heaven. (Ecclesiastes 3:1)

For every season of injustice, God looks for people who will respond to his call for justice. In his book *Issues Facing Christians Today*, John Stott reminds us that

> whenever God's people have been effective as salt and light in the community, there has been less social decay and more social uplift.
>
> In the United States, for example, after the early nineteenth-century awakening associated with Charles G. Finney, "born-again Christians were in the forefront of every major social reform in America. They spear-headed the abolitionist movement, the

temperance movement, the peace movement, and the early feminist movement."[2]

John Wesley is best remembered for his preaching, through which he influenced the church to challenge and change society. He fought to stop the cruelty and torture of animals. He fought against the African slave trade. He fought against the kidnapping of fellow countrymen by slave traders. He was a voice against gambling, prostitution, corruption, and many other evils and injustices of his day. As a result, Wesley was called both a preacher of the gospel and a prophet for social righteousness.[3]

We know William Wilberforce best for the ending of the trans-Atlantic slave trade, but he was also a social reformer. He was nicknamed "the prime minister of a cabinet of philanthropists"[4] and was at one time actively supporting sixty-nine causes. He gave away 25 percent of his income to the poor. He fought to keep young boys from being forced to work dangerous jobs in harmful conditions, like chimney sweeping. He sought educational reform to provide all children with regular education in reading, personal hygiene and religion. He fought to create agricultural reform to help provide affordable food for the poor. He influenced prison reform and the restriction of capital punishment from misuse. He helped support single moms, Sunday schools and orphanages. And he started groups like the Church Missionary Society, the British and Foreign Bible Society, and the Anti-Slavery Society.[5]

This is in our history as the church. And God is once again calling forth his church to lead the way into justice and righteousness. God is doing something globally about the injustice of modern-day slavery today. If you would have asked me just a few years ago about human trafficking, I would have looked at you as if you were speaking a foreign language. But within the past couple of years, we have seen this issue rise up in widespread awareness, and thankfully so.

In his book *The Meeting of the Waters*, Fritz Kling writes about his journey across the globe to see what the Spirit of God was doing in churches around the world, listing his top seven findings in global trends. The number one trend he saw was a movement toward mercy and social justice.

> In the coming years, respect and relevance will flow to the global church when it does what it was created to do: to fill gaping holes, both spiritual and physical, in the lives of unnoticed, unwanted people. This is the heart language of the next generation, non-Christians and Christians alike, and it is the first Global Current—Mercy.[6]

The speed at which this justice movement is growing is beyond human orchestration, and if the favor that God is giving to people involved in this movement is any indication, it reveals that this issue has been heavy on the Lord's heart for a long time. He has been waiting for his body to rise up and represent his love at this hour. The time is now for the church to step into this fight and move its way to the frontlines where we belong!

The Spirit is leading the church to declare and demonstrate the gospel to the darkest places in our cities, and we must respond with faith, obedience, courage, wisdom, humility and love.

> The greatest danger is that the valuable treasure carried by the church—the best news the world can ever hear—will be risked because leaders lack the stomach, mind, or heart to engage the changing times.[7]

I end this chapter with the story of Buri, our former administrative staff who risked her mind, heart and even her "guts" (in terms of fear!) to pursue the active call of the gospel. Months before I received the same calling from God, this young Korean woman with whom I had worked every day for years had secretly received a stirring in her heart for victims of trafficking.

Several years ago, some members of the International House of Prayer had visited Seoul and given words of encouragement for our staff. Buri was encouraged by their words to her, but she was also told that God would use her someday to help those who were trafficked. At first, she was confused—she'd never even heard the word "trafficking" before. She had to ask another staff person what the word meant. But Buri especially had a heart for five- to thirteen-year-old children. She wondered how these passions would all connect with her future. Her first thought was fear: *What if I run into organized crime? What if I get attacked? How can I get involved in such a dark world?*

But the following year was filled with an explosion of events—our first justice conference, the Backyard Academy, my sermons on justice—and Buri began learning more. Still, she viewed it as part of her administrative job. She had no idea how God wanted to use her. And secretly, she felt a bit afraid, lacking the stomach to take the step to find out. Later, she admitted that she never would have visited Thailand had I not required all of our staff to take a short-term missions trip. Soon after that trip, Buri volunteered to visit Kru Nam, a Thai woman who shelters approximately 140 children who have been rescued from sex trafficking. Located in Chang Mai near the border with Myanmar, Kru Nam is a modern-day hero who has dedicated her life to rescuing children trapped in the sex industry.

All the while, Buri really hesitated to go. To be honest, she felt burdened with self-consciousness and awkwardness, especially when she had to sing and dance before the kids. She joked later, "I felt like I was forcing my body to move, not even thinking about worship!" She didn't feel comfortable in front of all these children whom she didn't really know. But as the days passed, she started to feel a deep love and compassion for these children. She didn't want to leave.

As she was packing her bags on the last day, Buri heard someone calling her name. She turned to see sixty children running toward her, shouting, laughing and crying out her name. They all held out pieces of paper. They wanted her to write down her address so that they could stay in contact with her. Many tears were shed. Buri's heart broke. She started looking into the eyes of these children, and her life changed forever.

Then God spoke to her. He said, "I not only want you to be a light of hope for the victims of trafficking, I want you to be a witness and a missionary to these kids." God wanted Buri to see these *smiles*—the hope, the promise—of what he could do in this land.

Since then, Buri has committed her life to rescuing and restoring children who have been trafficked so that they might find true freedom through the love of Jesus Christ.

If you don't want to see the church involved in this issue, you can simply close your eyes and turn away. But those who realize that this is part of the gospel call will see darkness flee as the light of Jesus shines forth.

GROUP DISCUSSION QUESTIONS

- Define the gospel in your own words. How much of the gospel should be what we say versus what we do?

- Put into your own words why the church should be involved in this fight for justice.

- Do you believe the church should be leading this movement? Why or why not?

PRAYER GUIDE

- Ask God to give you a greater understanding and appreciation of the gospel of Jesus Christ.

- Pray that the church will rise up and lead the way toward justice as we live out the gospel in our lives.

- Ask God to get you and your church on mission with him.

WHAT THE CHURCH CAN DO

*In the same way, let your light shine before others,
so that they may see your good works and give
glory to your Father who is in heaven.*

Matthew 5:16

*Lack of citizenship is the
chief factor in the particular vulnerability
of hill tribe women and girls to trafficking
and other forms of exploitation.*

UNESCO

*All that is necessary for the triumph of evil
is that good men do nothing.*

Edmund Burke

A JUSTICE MINISTRY IS BORN: HOPE BE RESTORED

In 2010, when I first became aware of human trafficking, how our church could get involved in practical ways started popping into my mind during my brainstorming sessions with God. My anger against the injustice started turning into excitement because of the possibilities. I let these soak in prayer for a few weeks, and on December 24, 2010, HOPE Be Restored was born. This would become the freedom and justice ministry of our church, pioneering a new movement for Korea. Now before I share what HOPE Be Restored (HBR) does, I want to share about the significance of the name.

HOPE Be Restored stands for "Helping the Oppressed and Prisoners of injustice Escape and Be Restored." Our aim is to help, heal and restore lives through the power of God's love and the gospel of Jesus Christ. But more importantly, it is a declaration. It declares to this world that hope will be restored. It is a verbal declaration of faith of what we believe will be the end result in our world. We believe that those who live in hopelessness will find hope again. We are declaring by faith that hope will rise up out of the darkest night.

There are six key areas that we focus on.

1. RELEASING INTERCESSORS (PRAYER TEAM)

Ending human trafficking begins with prayer. The more I pray about this issue, the more I realize that the first line of battle must be fought on our knees. This is a spiritual issue, and it must be fought in the spiritual realm. Prayer has great power because it takes us into the presence of God. Prayer is the means through which God chooses to release his power into the world. Therefore, we believe prayer is a vital part of ending modern-day slavery.

As a result, the first "team" in our justice ministry is our prayer team. This team is dedicated to praying for the injustices to end and for people to be set free. But their role is also to find ways to increase prayers from the church and to help people pray more effectively. The HBR prayer team creates prayer guides to aid the church. We felt convicted that we must not only pray in our homes and in our churches, but also on the streets of our city. So our prayer teams participate in weekly and monthly prayer walks throughout the city. We do prayer and fasting chains for extended periods of time, sometimes up to forty days, because we understand the intense spiritual nature of the war that we are fighting.

In all this, we are seeking to tear down the spiritual strongholds that are connected to human trafficking, such as greed, lust and pride. Our prayer team is the cornerstone of this ministry because prayer keeps us connected to Christ, and Christ is the cornerstone for the church.

2. RAISING AWARENESS (AWARENESS TEAM)

Having established our prayer team, the next logical step was to create an awareness team. Human trafficking has gained a lot of attention in recent years, but there are still many who are either unaware or have misconceptions about modern-day slavery. So the awareness team works within our community—elementary schools, middle schools, high schools, colleges, churches, military bases and pretty much any place that is willing to hear what we have to say. Our church has been hosting an annual justice conference to raise awareness and equip churches to join the fight for justice. We also partner with several aftercare centers to hold campaigns in the streets of Seoul to let the public know what is happening to the millions of trafficked victims around the world. Though the journey toward justice begins with awareness for most, it must not end there.

David Batstone, the cofounder and president of Not for Sale, first encountered slavery in his own backyard when he discovered in the newspaper that his favorite Indian restaurant in San Francisco shut down after the police discovered the restaurant was using trafficked children to serve the tables and work in the kitchen. This shocking discovery led him on a journey around the world to find out how widespread slavery was. After months of research and interviews, he realized that he could no longer live life as usual while millions were enslaved. As a result, *Not for Sale* was written and a new organization to end slavery was born.[1] Awareness can be a powerful tool to open eyes and change the course of a life.

3. RESEARCH AND INVESTIGATION (RESEARCH TEAM)

In order to raise awareness effectively, we need good data to support our message. So we formed a team committed to researching trafficking cases within our city. They monitor trends and map key areas where trafficking happens. With this data, we know where we should be praying and what we should be praying for, thereby aiding our prayer team. The research team collects stories of victims and statistics from newspapers and police reports, compiling them into reports for the public to use. They are also able to help our awareness team with the most recent and relevant information to share during awareness campaigns. The research team also inputs trafficking cases into a database that documents convictions that happen around the world.

4. RELATIONSHIP BUILDING AND NETWORKING (NETWORKING TEAM)

Another key component of our ministry is building relationships with strategic partners who can help us bring an end to these injustices. We network with churches, government officials, law enforcement, lawyers, CEOs, celebrities and other organizations who share our passion to end slavery. It is amazing how well networked traffickers are with other industries, such as travel agents, border patrol, taxi drivers and even grocery store owners. If traffickers know how to network and work well with others, how much more does the church! We need to partner with each other and pool our resources together. We are in this together and need each other if we're going to see this evil end within our lifetime.

Currently, we are forming a global alliance of Christian

abolitionists called RAFA (Restoration Alliance of Faith-based Abolitionists) so that we can begin networking more effectively across the nations. You can email justice@onnurienglish .org if you'd like to join or get more information.

5. RESTORATION AND HEALING (RESTORATION TEAM)

A central part of our mission is to help restore hope and bring healing through the gospel of Jesus Christ. We believe the gospel must be declared and demonstrated. People must hear about God's love, but they also need to experience God's love through his body—the church.

Through prayer, counseling and friendships, we offer safe houses and aftercare centers to help the people we serve heal physically, emotionally and spiritually. These places also provide new job skills and educational opportunities so that they have the tools they need to build a bright new chapter in their lives.

We also have a House of Hope restoration center, where both victims and aftercare workers can come and spend time away from the daily grind and be refreshed in a secluded area surrounded by creation. We are committed to bringing help, healing, restoration and hope to all who are involved in this process of setting the captives free.

6. RESCUE AND PREVENTION (OUTREACH TEAM)

We not only want to rescue victims, we also want to prevent injustice from recurring. We partner with experienced aftercare workers to build relationships with sex trafficking victims in order to let them know that there are people ready to help them at a moment's notice. We also go to areas of high vulnerability, both in Korea and in other countries, in order to educate young children and women and to protect them before they fall into the hands of traffickers. This part of our ministry also engages in the battle for their freedom through prayer, fasting, evangelism, education, resource development and job creation.

WHAT CAN WE DO?

The most common question I receive from pastors and church leaders is, "What can we do as a church?"

There's a lot you can do! In fact, you have one of the most important roles to play in the abolition of modern-day slavery. As we've clearly seen, slavery is at its core a spiritual issue that must be dealt with in the spiritual realm. If you are a spiritual leader, this is your battleground. If God leads, I encourage you to begin a justice ministry in your church that has one or more components of the ideas found within this chapter.

Here is a list of ways that we the church can be involved, lead the way and bring an end to the injustice of human trafficking today.

TEACH AND PREACH

Sermons. The power of pulpit ministry must be utilized to raise up a new generation of abolitionists who are grounded in Scripture, persistent in prayer and willing to follow in the footsteps of Jesus. Provide the biblical groundwork for the congregation to know that this is a battle for the church to be engaged in. The issues we are up against concerning human trafficking are core spiritual issues, such as the greed that lures traffickers into this arena, the lust of the johns and the self-hatred that overcomes many victims.

To help get your congregation on board, I recommend doing a sermon series on human trafficking and modern-day slavery. A series on trafficking could encompass topics such as *love* for our neighbors, *lust* that enslaves, *mercy* toward the weak, *missions* needed in the darkest places of the world, *compassion* for the suffering, *freedom* for spiritual captives, *justice* as an expression of love, *slavery* that is not just physical bondage but also spiritual and emotional bondage, *greed* as a source of all kinds of evil, and how true love and freedom can be found in the mission, message and person of Jesus Christ.

Freedom Sunday. If preaching a series seems too daunting of a task to begin with, I encourage your church to start with Freedom Sunday (www.freedomsunday.org), which designates one Sunday out of the year to remember the millions around the world who are in physical and spiritual bondage. Be it through a sermon or a series, the preacher has a crucial role to play in casting a vision for being a light in this generation of darkness. (Please see the appendix to see a sample sermon on social justice.)

STUDY (PERSONAL AND GROUP)

Small group Bible studies. Doing a small group Bible study on the various issues connected to human trafficking (freedom, justice, mercy, bondage, etc.) can help get your church to study the issue biblically and discuss ways to take action within your community. Going through the discussion questions and prayers at the end of each chapter in this book can also be an effective tool for small groups. Doing a word study on "justice" throughout Scripture will reveal so much of God's heart for the weak and the oppressed, making it clear that the church is to be a reflection of that heart to our world. You can find more recommended books and resources to use for group studies in the appendix section of this book.

Studying history. From looking at the exodus account in Scripture to exploring the work of William Wilberforce in abolishing the British slave trade, studying the history of past abolitionist movements is another way to raise awareness and gain inspiration from freedom fighters who have gone before us. (See appendix for a list of books you can read.)

Screening films. There are some excellent documentaries that give an overview of human trafficking and include inspirational testimonies of what God is doing to set people free. Two in particular that I would recommend are *Nefarious: Merchant of Souls* by Exodus Cry and *At the End of Slavery: The Battle for Justice in Our Time* by IJM. Having movie nights or incorporating these films into a conference setting can be a powerful tool in raising awareness.

PRAYER

There are many ways that justice flows from God's throne into our world. It can come through the judicial systems of the world. It can come through law enforcement. But another way we are to seek justice is through persistent, faith-filled prayers to the God of justice. Bethany Hoang of International Justice Mission reminds us that "at the end of the day, if our attempts to seek justice do not first begin with the work of prayer, we will be worn and weary."[2]

> And he told them a parable to the effect that they ought always to pray and not lose heart. He said, "In a certain city there was a judge who neither feared God nor respected man. And there was a widow in that city who kept coming to him and saying, 'Give me justice against my adversary.' For a while he refused, but afterward he said to himself, 'Though I neither fear God nor respect man, yet because this widow keeps bothering me, I will give her justice, so that she will not beat me down by her continual coming.'" And the Lord said, "Hear what the unrighteous judge says. And will not God give justice to his elect, who cry to him day and night? Will he delay long over them? I tell you, he will give justice to them speedily. Nevertheless, when the Son of Man comes, will he find faith on earth?" (Luke 18:1-8)

The ultimate answer to our prayers for justice is the return of Jesus, the righteous judge who *will* make right all wrongs.

Prayer is a powerful weapon in the fight for freedom. Jesus tells us that it is through persistent, faith-filled prayer that God will bring forth justice to his elect (Luke 18:7). Much of the heavy fighting takes place in the unseen arena of spiritual warfare. Prayer changes things, and it is prayer that can bring transformation in the spiritual dimension of a community.

International Justice Mission understands the utter importance of prayer, so they begin their workdays with thirty minutes of silence and prayer and then gather again at eleven o'clock to pray.[3] I don't think it is a coincidence that they have seen so many breakthroughs in trafficking cases around the world and favor from influential supporters. Therefore, I strongly encourage everyone in the church to pray on a regular basis for the end of human trafficking in our lifetime.

Give your church some practical steps on how to pray for this issue. The list of items to pray for can become quite extensive, but I want to highlight several topics that you can begin with.

Pray for the victims. Pray for all who are bound physically and spiritually to be set free, and pray that they will be healed and restored in Jesus' name.

Pray for the traffickers. Pray that they would repent of their sins and turn from their wicked ways. Pray that they too would be set free from their bondage to greed and pursue the greatest treasure—Jesus Christ.

Pray for justice in the justice system. Since corruption is a major factor that allows trafficking to happen globally, pray that those in positions of power and influence would do the right thing and uphold the law to protect the vulnerable. Pray that justice would reign in the law enforcement and judicial systems of the world.

Pray for the "breaking grounds" to be destroyed. The breaking grounds are one of the darkest and most hideous places on the planet. It is where victims of sex trafficking are "seasoned" for the profession of prostitution through sexual assault, physical abuse and drugs. Pray that the police will find these places and every breaking ground would disappear from this planet in Jesus' name.

Pray for organizations on the frontlines. Pray for protection, provision and success for groups around the world that fight on behalf of the oppressed. Pray for effectiveness as they seek to educate, rescue and restore the vulnerable. Pray that they would be strengthened with joy for their difficult journey of seeing justice established in places where corruption often runs rampant.

Pray for the church to rise up. Pray that the church would awaken from its slumber over justice issues and become the leading force in declaring and demonstrating the gospel to a world in darkness.

Pray for more intercessors. Pray that God will raise up more people to pray and intercede for justice to be established in every nation. Pray that God will raise up prayer houses in your city. Pray that God will raise up intercessors who will contend in the place of prayer, night and day, until the captives are set free.

Repent for the sins we have committed. Pray prayers of repentance for the ways that we have sinned by our lust, our greed and our selfishness. Confess the sins of the church and of our nation. Before we condemn the sinner "over there," let us confess the sins in our own hearts.

Pray for the end of human trafficking and modern-day slavery. Let us be specific and intentional about praying for the end of this great evil and injustice in our lifetime. We do not want to leave this evil as an inheritance to the next generation.

It is important to get your church to pray for this issue. A key question to ask is, "How can we increase prayer?" Here are some suggestions:

Partner with your prayer ministry. One of the most important ministries to have involved in this movement for freedom and justice is your church's prayer ministry. There is power in prayer, and as more prayers go up, more strongholds will come down. While we want everyone praying for freedom and justice, it is wise to begin with those gifted with intercession and those who have a heart for prayer.

Prayer walk in your community. Our church has a monthly prayer walk where we go to key areas of influence in our city (city hall, supreme court, etc.) and pray against injustice and for blessings in our community. We also send more seasoned and experienced intercessory teams to pray in areas of darkness or areas known for sex trafficking, but extreme wisdom, caution and supervision is strongly recommended before sending anyone to a potentially dangerous area. This is intense spiritual warfare, so be prayerful and careful as you follow God's lead concerning this area.

Last year, several of our church members did a prayer walk through Gangnam every second and fourth Tuesday. The area is a lively spot for night life with hidden, unassuming venues where sex trafficking often occurs. The sidewalks are littered with small business cards and flyers for massage parlors, adult internet cyber rooms and room salons. One of the members reported this: "Not long into it, we noticed a profound decline in prostitution ads on the ground in the area. And it came to our attention that there had been a huge bust on the people printing those ads. Praise God! Also, a few months into praying for the area, it was seen in the news that the city had ordered a mass investigation into the loan sharks of Gangnam, something that we had been praying for specifically and extensively." Prayer walks bear fruit, so keep walking and keep praying!

Join a 24/7 prayer chain. Your church can create its own prayer chain for justice or join prayer groups that are already engaged in this. If you would like to join our church's 24/7 prayer chain, you can email justice@onnurienglish.org. You can also join in Exodus Cry's prayer sessions on human trafficking at their website www.exoduscry.com.

The Red Light Initiative. I love this idea that was created by Exodus Cry. Each time you are waiting at a red light in your car, pray for the removal of the red-light districts in your city, community and country. Pray for the victims of sex trafficking to be set free and healed.

FASTING

A biblical fast. Isaiah 58 tells us that our fasting should not be about just giving up our food but also feeding others who are without food. It is a time to seek justice within our lives and within our communities. Verse 6 of the chapter says, "Is not this the fast that I choose: to loose the bonds of wickedness, to undo the straps of the yoke, to let the oppressed go free, and to break every yoke?"

A God-honoring fast is not just giving up something I need, it also means seeking to meet the needs of those who are oppressed within our world. It is choosing to suffer in this small way so that I might gain a heart of compassion for the sufferings of others. Here are a few types of fasting that you might consider practicing:

Personal fast. I know many people who have been led by God to do an extended period of personal fasting for the sins of the nation and the freedom of captives. Whether it is one meal, one day or longer, pray that our longing for food would be replaced by a greater longing for justice.

Corporate fast. During the season of Lent, our church goes through a "Fast for Freedom." This a forty-day fast of giving up one meal per day, Monday to Saturday, from Ash Wednesday to Easter Sunday. During this fast, instead of eating a meal, we spend time praying for the captives and remembering the suffering that they are going through.

In addition to giving up one meal per day, we set aside the money we would have used on that meal and donate it to a freedom project. Our first "Fast for Freedom" raised about $75,000 and we were able to give that money to help buy land and build a new dorm for children in Northern Thailand who are survivors of human trafficking. During another campaign, the money raised went toward college scholarships for stateless children in Northern Thailand.

Slavery-made fast. Another idea is to have the church fast from slavery-made foods and products. See which products within stores are made in a way that dishonors life and fast from those companies until changes are made. Free2Work (www.free2work.org) can help you learn more about where companies stand in terms of proper work practices in their supply chain.

OTHER CHURCH MINISTRIES THAT CAN GET INVOLVED

Men's ministry. In June 2011, we hosted a conference that focused on training people in practical ways to combat trafficking. At one of the workshops we held during this three-day event, a man in the audience raised his hand and asked, "What can men do to help stem this tide of sex trafficking?" The workshop leader, a woman with decades of experience in the field, didn't bat an eye. "Stop watching pornography," she said. The consumption of porn and prostitution is fueled by lust, and for men that starts not only in the privacy of their home computer but within their hearts.

Involvement in justice work not only spurs men to greater personal holiness because they witness the direct impact that lust has on women around the world, but it also provides a positive focal point for realizing that to break the chains of human trafficking in this world, men need to learn how to be men of God.

Filmmaker Ryan Abella, who helped us create videos to raise awareness about human trafficking in South Korea, became so inspired when he sifted through the moving testimonies of trafficked women that he wrote a blog post titled "Break the Chains—Be a Man." Ryan wrestled with what he could do about this overwhelming problem:

> I've battled this question for most of my adult life, whether the dollar I give to an organization makes a real difference or whether a simple act of kindness translates to a better world. The thing is . . . it does help. Positive change starts with small steps. Even for something like sex trafficking, we have somewhere to start. All of us do, both men and women: If we're to break the chains of human trafficking in this world, men need to learn what it means to be men.

Ryan is right. Though many women's ministries (and prayer ministries) are the first to express interest in combating trafficking, especially sex trafficking, the men's ministries of churches have an important role to play as well. Sadly, it is the men who, for the most part, drive the demand for sex trafficking through the consumption of pornography or attaining prostitution services.

If we want to root out the demand, we need to help men become who God intended them to be. Instead of being enslaved to porn and sexual perversion, the heart needs an encounter with the gospel of Jesus Christ so that it will be free to honor sex as a gift to be enjoyed within the marriage covenant between husband and wife.

So what can a men's ministry do?

- *Provide accountability.* In a world where sexually provocative images are on display wherever we look, men need a place to share struggles and find support. Having one-to-one mentoring or small groups of accountability will be a great gift to offer the men of your church. Let them form their own antiporn community and fight for purity and honor together.

- *Mobilize and mentor men of valor.* Creating a new culture where purity and fidelity is honored is bringing the kingdom of God into your church. Men of valor who will be courageous and strong are needed, who seek to defend the weak and oppressed. For far too long, we have allowed Hollywood and *Playboy* to define what a man looks like. We need a new generation of men committed to Christ and his word to show the next generation that Jesus is the ultimate definition of manhood. Have godly men mentor younger men in your church and teach them that they were created to be a source of protection for women, not supporters of exploitation. It is time to disciple the boys to be true men in Christ.

- *Share the gospel with the men of your city.* Hearts can only change through the power of the gospel, and we need to offer the good news to every man, woman and child in our cities. Since men are driving the demand for sex trafficking around the world, when the hearts of men change, this situation will change. Share the gospel today and let us pray for a revival among the men in our generation.

Women's ministry. I encourage women to consider volunteering at local aftercare centers, since the victims are often women. There are a vast number of ways women can be involved through prayer, fundraising and even mentoring the younger girls in your community.

Last December, some women from our praise team volunteered to knit scarves for some women at Duraebang—the shelter for migrant woman in sex trafficking that is located in Pyeongtaek. Although some of the members on our team didn't know how to knit, they gathered together, taught each other the basic skills they needed, and then traveled together to present the scarves they made as Christmas gifts. Several of the women in Duraebang were from the Philippines. They had been tricked into thinking they were working for legitimate businesses in South Korea and were now in hiding. They received the scarves with beaming smiles and such joyful gratitude.

And, as mentioned, one of the other local women's shelters we partner with is called EcoGender. Whether it's teaching

English to the staff, helping to sell flower pots for fundraising, or collecting clothing, shoes and toys, we've found various ways to partner with them. Several of the women from my church have led the way in maintaining regular contact with EcoGender, helping them network and connecting them with resources, sometimes on a weekly basis. They have also supported them for events.

One huge event last year was during Easter. Several of us helped to decorate eggs for EcoGender so they could give them out to the sisters at Yongjugal. While we were making the eggs, we knew that it might all be in vain because, up until that point, the sisters had been prohibited from accepting any food from outside sources. The pimps had told them lies about the food and made them afraid.

So they never before had ever accepted food from Eco-Gender. We prayed hard over these eggs! We prayed Easter into them so that they would sow the seeds of new life into these women's lives. After Easter, we got word from EcoGender that for the first time ever, the women accepted the eggs! Ever since, EcoGender has been able to give out baked goods and treats to the sisters, and now even the pimps. Praise God!

Family ministry. A vast number of women in South Korea who end up sex trafficked or in prostitution come from a broken family background. They come from divorced parents or single parent homes. The emotional disconnect they experience at home will drive many young girls to the streets where they sometimes fall prey to traffickers. Establishing a strong family ministry in the church can serve as a preventative measure by keeping families together and keeping children off the streets. Parents need to understand there are so many blessings that children gain from a loving family upbringing, but so much potential for harm and heartbreak from families that split apart. Let us pray for healing and health in our families today.

Orphan care ministry. Orphans are one of the most vulnerable people in the world to fall into the hands of traffickers. With no one looking out for them, especially after they leave the institutional system, they are left to fend for themselves. In some countries, traffickers wait until girls "age out" of the orphanages and recruit them for their own businesses. Establishing a church ministry that cares for the orphan through foster care, adoption and mentoring programs is another way to not only love the vulnerable with the love of Jesus but also protect a group of people who are often a target for traffickers.

Recently, a local orphanage ran out of funds and had to close down. One of the workers at the orphanage knew that our church had a heart for orphans. He contacted me asking if anyone in our church could become foster parents for one of their twelve-year-old girls who had nowhere to go. I already knew too well that sending a twelve-year-old girl with no family support onto the streets was a trafficking story waiting to happen, so without even asking our church members, I told him that I guaranteed someone in our church would care for her. I called one couple in our community, Kent and Daisy

Lee, explained the situation and asked if they'd be willing to be foster parents for this young girl. They prayed about it for a day and the next afternoon they called me saying that they would care for her. I was overjoyed at their quick response. Orphan care in the church is a vital part of loving our neighbors, valuing the vulnerable and preventing tragic stories from happening.

Youth group. Take advantage of the passion that teens have and release them to use that energy to raise awareness of trafficking. This generation of youth is wired to live their lives with purpose and to respond passionately to help others. I have provided a few awareness and fundraising ideas that your youth group can use in the awareness section listed later in this chapter.

Children's ministry. I used to think that our children's ministry was too young to understand the issues of justice and freedom, but I was wrong. Children know what is right, wrong and fair. Teaching them about sex trafficking is probably not a good idea, but telling them about child slave labor is something that they can connect with.

I had the opportunity to share how children in Africa are sometimes victims of slave labor and are forced to pick cocoa beans, which in turn are used to make many of our chocolates. I showed them the grades that some of the biggest brand-name chocolate companies received for this slavery practice within their supply chain from the Free2Work website (www .free2work.org). The result of the simple talk? One of the fifth grade girls named Esther compiled a list of all the grades that the chocolate companies received and she distributed it to all of her classmates at school. Esther and her friends then decided not to buy slavery-made chocolate anymore. I do not know if I could have done that as a young fifth grader myself, but I was proud to see how, at such a young age, she not only understood the issue, she took a stand and became a voice for these African children. Now we have a bunch of fifth grade abolitionists who are already influencing their generation! You can see a copy of her chocolate report card at the HOPE Be Restored website (www.hopeberestored.org).

Single moms ministry. It may not be the case for all countries, but at least in South Korea where I minister, the young single mom population is growing, and they are vulnerable. There are currently over two hundred thousand young single moms with children under the age of eighteen. Most say that financial difficulty is their biggest challenge, with the average monthly income ranging between five hundred and one thousand dollars. The Ministry of Health and Welfare did a survey in 2012 that showed that most of these moms have to borrow money each month in order to make ends meet, and 22 percent borrow three hundred to one thousand dollars per month for living costs. Because of the increasing debts they face each month, a large number give up their children for adoption even though they don't want to. They simply can't afford to keep their child. And even if they give up their children, they are still faced with a large debt that they must somehow pay off.

We discovered that because of the debt many of these moms incur, and the limited education they have (most do not have a high school education), they are unable to get a proper loan from banks. In times of desperation, they often have to turn to loan sharks who add on a large amount of interest (sometimes more than 300%!). Getting deeper and deeper into debt, some of these women are forced into the sex industry as a means of paying back their creditors.

One of the most heartbreaking things our teams have reported during their prayer walks and visits to the red-light districts are the scattered toys and children's clothes hanging outside the brothels. One of our members said,

> There was also the toy stores and children's clothes in Yongjugal (a red-light district) that are on display and sometimes seen in the brothels themselves. In that, I saw how these women are still trying to have a normal life, how they're still trying love their children.

So as another preventative measure to care for this vulnerable group (both for the moms and the orphans), our church began a ministry called Single Love that provides free diapers, baby clothes, food, child care, tutoring help, mentoring and friendships so that these young moms can be encouraged to keep going and dream great dreams for themselves and their children.

In January 2013, we held a fundraiser in Seoul where we raised sixty million won (over $50,000) for the House of Hope.

The House of Hope is a new building that will be the first gospel-centered safe house in South Korea. This two-story, twelve-bedroom building will provide shelter, counseling and restoration for single pregnant mothers and victims of sex trafficking. The Women's Hope Center (WHC) will manage the House of Hope in collaboration with OEM's HOPE Be Restored. Construction of the building is set to begin this year thanks in part to a generous donation of two hundred pyeong (660 square meters) of land in a location outside of Andong. This new building will also have a crisis pregnancy shelter and a sex trafficking restoration center for women who have left the sex industry and are struggling to adjust back into society.

Such projects like the House of Hope are the result of a choice: we realized that we could either judge these women like the rest of the world, or we could love them like Jesus. We decided to love them.

Here's what one team member said about her experience reaching out to rescued foreign women at one of our partner aftercare centers:

> Frankly speaking, I did not have much idea of who the Duraebang women were until I met each of them in person. Besides knowing that most of them had come from the Philippines and that they were around my age, the rest of my perception, I'm ashamed to admit, relied upon social labels such as "immigrant," "foreigner," "victimized," "illegal" or "at-risk."

The first five minutes of our meeting were awkward. We seemed to have nothing in common externally—skin color, body type, language, favorite foods, culture, even gestures. It was clear that we came from two very different worlds. Since I didn't know how to break the ice, I did what I usually do in situations like this—I smiled and nodded a lot.

As time went on, however, one girl's story started to open my heart. Usually a story this emotionally taxing relieves my fear of building a relationship too quickly or in too lopsided a way—I didn't know where her sudden trust towards us came from, and I also didn't want her to regret later for so quickly showing her most vulnerable side. This time was different, however. Her bold story left my heart broken and vulnerable for her. As she was speaking, I could see how every word from her mouth struck me, and how I would keep and go over them in my heart.

The rest of the day was fun. We talked, laughed, sang Christmas songs, made crafts, cleaned, took many pictures, embraced, then bid each other good-bye.

Back in Seoul, I realized that these women had opened my eyes to free my ignorant views of at-risk women as merely the objects of sympathy, ignorance or indifference to an actual group of fellow women with whom I could share with, care for, and love.

I learned today that all of us should give ourselves a

chance to meet, serve, and simply spend time with people like the women in My Sister's Home.

I encourage you to look into your community and find out who the vulnerable people are. It may be the teen runaways, it may be the orphan, it may be the single moms. And instead of judging them, let's love them, serve them and help them have the best life possible as we show them the love and grace of Jesus.

MISSION PROJECTS

Short-term missions. Along with traditional short-term mission trips, our church also provides opportunities to go on mission trips that serve organizations that are on the frontlines in this fight for freedom. From providing English lessons to doing vacation Bible school to simply cleaning the facilities, serving those who are rescuing and restoring survivors of trafficking is always an honor. YWAM (Youth with a Mission) also provides a Discipleship Training School program that has a justice track for its outreach. Those who would like to commit to several months of service can consider this option.

Long-term missions. For churches who are actively engaged in sending out long-term missionaries and establishing crosscultural church plants overseas, I suggest you prayerfully consider planting churches in regions of the world where trafficking frequently happens. It is in these dark places that the light of the body of Christ needs to be established.

Our church is currently praying about church planting in Isaan, the northeastern part of Thailand. Some surveys have shown that up to 80 percent of the women working in the red-light districts of Thailand are from this region. Also, some parts of Eastern Europe, such as Moldova, are experiencing a major orphan crisis due to economic instability, leading many young children and girls to fall into the trafficking industry. It would be wonderful to see churches show up in these places, leading the way in providing safety and solutions.

Above all else, wherever you see great darkness in the hearts of men, the light of the gospel needs to be all the more present. We need to continually plant churches and worship in dark places.

CASE STUDY: AGAPE INTERNATIONAL MISSIONS

Agape International Missions (AIM) is a pioneer in the fight against sex trafficking in Cambodia. Don Brewster, the founder and director of AIM, realized that the only way to drive out darkness was to bring the light and love of Jesus into these dark communities. This church decided it needed to live in areas where trafficking was happening and become a part of the community. As a result, they were able to befriend the locals and gather crucial information that has led to the rescue and restoration of hundreds of girls in their area. Three key things they do are fight trafficking, restore victims and transform communities.

One key way they fight trafficking is through The Lord's

Gym, which is a free workout center where their staff builds relationships with traffickers. As relationships are formed, they have opportunities to share the good news of the gospel and the evil of trafficking, and they invite traffickers to attend church and receive prayer. Here is a powerful testimony of what happened to one trafficker after his time in The Lord's Gym.

Sokunthy was notorious for trafficking young girls. Every day, he attended The Lord's Gym where he was prayed for by the staff, heard the truth about the evil he was perpetuating within the community, and was invited to church. One day, AIM was called to help two very young girls who had been raped by their brother. It was Sokunthy. When he didn't come to the gym the following day, AIM's pastor went and told him, "You know we hate what you did. But the truth is, the gym is the Lord's gym. And no matter what you've done He'll forgive you. We want you to come back." He came back the next day, agreeing to go to church. Once there, he stood up and said, "I know what I was doing was wrong, and I am never going to do it again." AIM discipled him and helped him get a new job. There, he makes a clean $50 a month compared to the thousands he would make in trafficking. Through the power of prayer and the working of God's Holy Spirit, he has not hurt another child and is completely transformed.[4]

Another way they fight trafficking is through an anti-trafficking training program they offer to the church body. It is an eight-session workshop that offers ways to create a prevention plan, cut off the supply and confront the demand, and strategies for aftercare. You can request training in your own church by visiting their website: http://agapewebsite.org /projects/aim-anti-trafficking-training.

The second part of their ministry is restoring the victims of sex trafficking through their Agape Restoration Center (ARC) and the Agape Training Center (ATC). The ARC is where they seek to meet the physical, psychosocial, educational, vocational and spiritual needs of those rescued. They are given a safe place to live, nutritious meals, counseling, therapy, education, job skills and spiritual feeding for their holistic growth. The ATC provides new career opportunities for these young women to earn income and experience a new level of self-worth and dignity. Here is a testimony from someone who came out of the ARC:

> Mi arrived at ARC at the age of 12 after being sold by her mother and abused physically, sexually and emotionally for years. Through the loving guidance of Mi's counselors and house moms, hope blossomed in Mi's heart, and she accepted Jesus as her Lord. She applied herself in her academic studies and vocational training, landing a job in a high-profile bakery. Now she creates beautiful cakes for the Prime Minister and the King and

earns enough to support herself and her siblings. "I was so happy when I lived at ARC," Mi writes. "Although being at home there's many struggles, yet they motivate me to be firm and strong and persevere in dealing with my life circumstances. Every day when I come back from work I teach the poor kids in my community how to read and write so they can live good. I sacrificially lay out my lifestyle to help those kids like ARC helps me no matter how trivial my problem. Now I can help others, and I do it with everything I have and all of my heart."[5]

A third part of their strategy to fight trafficking is through transforming communities. They offer a Kid's Club that teaches literacy, English, life skills, Bible stories, arts, crafts and music to over four hundred children in their community. There is Rahab's House Church, a Christ-centered, Bible-teaching community church providing worship and discipleship. They also provide quality health care through a clinic that is available to all people in their community. And they have a community school that teaches reading, math, life skills and ESL.

The successful fruit of these ministries has resulted in church plants and church networks with over one thousand village churches throughout Cambodia. These are some of the ways that the gospel is demonstrated and declared there. The people have experienced the verbal and visible witness of the church. Lives are being saved and communities are being transformed because of it.

The exciting part about AIMs story is that every church can do similar ministries within their own community. We don't have to get on an airplane to do the mission that God has given us. We begin by being light wherever God has placed us to be. Research your community and find out who the vulnerable are and begin serving them. *The Just Church* by Jim Martin gives some practical advice on forming an action plan against the injustices of your community and how to engage your area for justice as a church.

SERVING THOSE ENSLAVED

Friendship. With wisdom and guidance from your pastor, I would also prayerfully see if the Lord is guiding some of the women in your church to befriend the women who are working in the red-light districts or other areas of prostitution in your communities. Please use caution depending on the safety risks involved. This type of ministry needs to be done by spiritually mature and sensitive people. I would not advise this for everyone, but I believe the Lord will guide some more women and churches to begin loving and befriending these women just like Jesus did.

Gift baskets. With the wisdom and approval of your pastor, as well as a leading from the Lord, consider giving gift baskets to women who are in the red-light districts of your city. These gift baskets will usually have toiletries and practical items as well as a small stuffed animal. There is a church in Houston that gives out care packages to women who are working in massage parlors where women have been trafficked. With the approval of the pimp, another church I know gave flowers to the women on Valentine's Day and Christmas.

CONNECT AND COLLABORATE

Network together. Bring together the various professions within your congregation and brainstorm to see what you can do as a networking freedom community. There are few places in the world that have such a diverse group of professions gathered together on a weekly basis like a church. There is great potential for synergy and creative ideas to come out of such a gathering, such as:

Resource provision. Take some of the entrepreneurial business members of your congregation on a vision trip to some of the poorer areas of the world where trafficking happens, and see what kind of business venture ideas they can come up with to create job opportunities for those who are vulnerable to traffickers. You never know what kind of great ideas will come from pooling resources together and brainstorming with God and his people.

I know of people who have donated their extra summer home to an aftercare center so that women who were victims of trafficking can have a safe place to stay during their restoration period. Others who own their own businesses or are CEOs of companies have offered entry-level jobs and job training to these survivors.

Network with other churches. Learn from other churches

that are taking steps in their community to fight trafficking. Also, join together with other churches to have a joint worship or prayer meeting to declare freedom in your city. That kind of unity would not only be a powerful witness to the world, it would also bring great delight to the Father's heart.

Vocational collaboration. In my church, our Korean-speaking congregation formed a group based on the Clapham Sect called the Christian CEO Forum. This group of high-level business leaders gathers together on a weekly basis for fellowship breakfasts, midweek discipleship and quarterly conferences to brainstorm solutions for the greatest levels of changes they can bring for the greatest good. You will find that when gifted leaders are given a problem, their natural bent toward problem solving can create some innovative solutions. Take advantage of how the leaders of your congregation are wired and bring them together to solve some of the greatest problems of our generation.

They don't have to be business leaders to have people from different professions work together to tackle this issue. For example, we have a lot of teachers in our congregation and they formed a Teachers Abolitionist Movement. One of the tools they created was a curriculum series to teach grade school, middle school and high school students about human trafficking and modern-day slavery. Students have also started clubs in their schools that raise awareness and do fundraising drives. We have lawyers who volunteer their services to help victims process their legal forms and inform them of their rights. Every profession can do something to change society for the better. This is what Jesus meant by being salt and light. It's about being a change agent in the place where God puts you.

Let the government hear the voice of the church. As a church filled with voters, push for legislation that protects victims and punishes traffickers. There is power in numbers, especially in the eyes of politicians, so let your voice be heard. Research which laws your local and national government has in place concerning human trafficking. If you are unsure where to start, contact organizations like Polaris Project or International Justice Mission (IJM). They have been leaders in the fight for justice through legislation advocacy. When the opportunity comes, have people sign petitions for law changes and declare your desire for justice. Even if things don't change right away, persevere and keep the issue on the public agenda. One of Wilberforce's greatest traits was his persevering spirit that would not give up, even after years of defeat, which kept this issue always before the British parliament.

Create neighborhood watch programs. As an individual believer, a small group or church, help bring the community together by raising awareness about hotlines they can call to report trafficking activity.

Boycott and buycott. During the trans-Atlantic slave trade, some of the Presbyterian churches in Scotland discovered that slaves were used in the production of the sugar that they used. So they began a boycott of sugar until slaves were no longer used. As a result of these churches coming together, more than three hundred thousand people stopped buying sugar! This affected the sugar industry and forced them to take a close look at their manufacturing process, not just the end product. Even today, most of the chocolate we buy is a product of slave labor, often by children who are forced to work the cocoa farms in Africa. We must look at tools such as Free2Work and see which companies honor their employees and which companies use slave labor. Not only must we boycott the companies who oppress their laborers, we need to support the companies that honor the dignity of their workers. We boycott the ones who oppress workers and "buycott" (a term I am borrowing from David Batstone) companies that work with integrity. Another way to strengthen our purchasing power is to buy (and/or sell) items made by freedom businesses and support the restoration of these survivors in their journey toward new life.

RAISING AWARENESS

I intentionally put raising awareness near the end of my list of suggestions, even though for most people, it would be the top item of what we need to do. While I agree that everyone needs to begin with awareness, I have seen how awareness can actually work against you if you do not have an action plan people can engage with already in place. In short, what I have learned is that *awareness without action leads to apathy*. People who know but do not do will quickly not care. Everyone needs to begin with becoming aware, but I encourage you to have a way for people to get involved in one or more of the areas listed in this chapter so that they will be a part of the solution.

Here are a few simple ways to raise awareness.

Social media and blogs. An easy way to help raise awareness within your own social circles is by simply blogging or posting stories on trafficking. Many friends become aware of issues and causes simply through the articles and news reports that get posted through social media.

My friend Tara Teng, who was Miss World Canada 2012, regularly posts on her Facebook and Twitter pages about human trafficking. On one occasion, after she posted about signs to look for to see if someone is being trafficked, a viewer realized that her father was using slave labor for the family restaurant. As difficult as it was to turn her own father in to the police, this girl knew it was the right thing to do. So she called the police, who investigated and discovered that her father was indeed guilty of labor trafficking. They planned a raid and rescued the young men and women from their imprisonment.

Campaigns. Awareness campaigns are a great way to let the community know that the body of Christ cares for people outside its four walls. Through walk-a-thons and bike-a-thons, every age group in the church can participate, bringing the church together and becoming a witness along the way. Some of these campaigns can also be used as fundraising events that will not only raise awareness but also collect money that can be used to support anti-trafficking organizations or aftercare centers.

Screenings. Public screenings of human trafficking films such as *Nefarious* provide a great way for people from the community to become aware of this issue and become familiar with your church. It's a movie night with a purpose.

Conferences. Hosting a conference and inviting an expert in this field, such as a representative from IJM, Love 146 or HOPE Be Restored, can help educate your church and inspire your group into action. Also, having your congregation attend national conferences held throughout the year is another option if you are unable to host your own.

Arts, books and media. Hannah More was an abolitionist during the trans-Atlantic slave trade in the nineteenth century who wrote poems against the slave trade. She also encouraged other women to use their skills to spread the message of what was happening to these victims. Suddenly a group of middle-class women played a key role in raising awareness. Some of them wrote plays that portrayed the realities of what was happening, others made paintings, some wrote children's books on the issue, and others wrote articles for newspapers and churches.

RESEARCH

One way to grow in personal awareness is to research and study the trafficking occurring within your own community. Through news reports, you can keep track of convictions and arrests connected to trafficking in your area and use that to guide your prayers. Here are some ideas to grow as a researcher.

Slavery map. Not for Sale created a tool called Slavery Map (www.slaverymap.org) that documents cases of human trafficking in all the cities of the world. It provides a quick way for people to see just how prevalent trafficking is in all parts of the globe. Those who have gone through their Investigator's Training can also upload data and add information connected to trafficking convictions that have occurred within your area. This becomes a very convincing advocacy tool especially when speaking with those who think that slavery "doesn't happen in my area."

Spiritual map. Just as Slavery Map is a valuable tool, the church can also map other spiritual strongholds within the community by creating a spiritual map of your neighborhoods. Print out a map of your area and highlight areas of influence (good or bad) that need to be kept in prayer. This can be a helpful aid to the prayer-walking teams that go from your church. Through it, you can also see how changes are happening in your community as you continue to pray.

AIM anti-trafficking training. Agape International Missions provides excellent training for the modern-day abolitionist through its anti-trafficking training program. They offer ways to learn more about creating a prevention plan for your church and ways to provide help for those rescued. These are high-quality forms of training for those who want to become effective abolitionists (http://agapewebsite.org/projects/aim -anti-trafficking-training).

Free2Work. As we've seen, many products we buy are the end result of slavery within a company's supply chain. An easy way to research which companies honor those who work for them and which do not is to look at the grades provided through the Free2Work smartphone app or their website (www.free2work.org). It provides a way that we can shop and eat to the glory of God by honoring the workers who made the products we consume possible.

Specialized research. We have a research team for our justice ministry that has been documenting trafficking cases connected to Koreans for the past several years. They not only input data into Slavery Map, but they also categorize their findings and turn it into a brief overview paper which has become a helpful resource for others to learn about trafficking in South Korea. As patterns and trends come up within our research, the way is paved for us to have more specialized research available. For example, a common theme among young girls who become trafficked for sex in South Korea is broken family backgrounds, which lead many of them to run away from home. So another research project our team is working on is the connection between runaways in Korea and trafficking. This will ultimately help families, counselors, youth pastors and others who work with children to realize what factors influence the vulnerability of children and how to help those who may end up on the streets. It will be an awareness and preventative tool.

GIVE TIME AND RESOURCES

Volunteer. Most aftercare centers and organizations that fight
human trafficking are non-profits with limited funding and
resources. Find out which groups are in your area and offer
to serve with them. We have taught English to some of the
staff members and survivors in one aftercare center. During
Christmas, we threw a party and gave gifts, thanking the staff
members for the wonderful work that they were doing. We
have had others volunteer their language and translation
skills to help Southeast Asian women who were trafficked
into South Korea fill out their legal documentation and apply
for work permits. We have taught women in other groups the
guitar, helped clean their offices and sometimes just baked
some cookies. These small acts of kindness and service have
allowed us to build good relationships with many aftercare
centers in South Korea. Please be understanding and gracious
if groups do not take you up on your offer to volunteer because of the sensitivity of the work they are involved with.
The protection and privacy of their victims must be guarded
well. If you or your church have limited resources, simply
offer your services to support and help other groups that are
already in this battle.

Give financially. Last, but not least, you can always give
your money to support groups that are doing the good work
of rescue, restoration and intervention. A little money can go
a long way in helping people who have lived through the
nightmare of human trafficking. Ten dollars in Cambodia will

allow a rescued girl to live in a shelter for over a week. A few hundred dollars can help a stateless student get a college education, opening a whole new world of opportunities. There are many great organizations to give to, and I've provided a list of some of them in the appendix of this book. Prayerfully seek how you and your church can give generously and make a world of difference in the lives of many.

This is by no means an exhaustive list of what churches can do in the fight against human trafficking, but it is a start. I hope you can use this list as a catalyst for action to get people involved. I also hope this can inspire more ideas to come out of the local church so that the universal church—the body of Christ—will one day take its rightful place on the frontlines in the fight for freedom and justice.

GROUP DISCUSSION QUESTIONS

- Which two or three ideas from this list do you feel you could begin doing right away?

- Which two or three ideas do you think your church can be involved with?

- What will you do now to make these ideas a reality within your life and ministry?

PRAYER GUIDE

- Ask God for wisdom, humility and courage to take the next steps of action.

- This is spiritual warfare, so take some time to pray for protection over yourself, your church and your pastor as you move into this area of justice.

- Pray for your church to be used by God to bring freedom and hope to your community.

CONCLUSION

The Time Is Now

Righteousness and justice
are the foundation of your throne;
steadfast love and faithfulness go before you.

Psalm 89:14

Human trafficking is now considered
the second largest and fastest growing illegal
trafficking activity in the world.

UN Office on Drugs and Crime

There are times to read history,
and there are times to make history.

David Batstone

TIME TO MAKE SLAVERY HISTORY

Slavery is not a thing of the past. With the tens of millions who are affected by this horror, there are *more* slaves today than at any other point in human history!

According to the Gospel Coalition, almost 40 percent of all trafficking situations investigated by US law enforcement agencies between 2008 and 2010 "involved prostitution of a child or child sexual exploitation."[1] And a disproportion of overall child trafficking takes place in Asia where sex tourists—including those from wealthier Asian nations like Japan and South Korea—visit poorer countries where children are captured, sold and exploited for profit.

Edmund Burke once said, "All that is necessary for the triumph of evil is that good men do nothing." After all this—seeing the magnitude and scope of the evil of human trafficking—we can easily become discouraged to the point of feeling utterly helpless. But there is hope because light is always greater than darkness. It is a law of nature in the physical world that points us to the greater reality in the spiritual realm. As light is always greater than darkness, love is stronger than hatred. In the end, good will triumph over evil and the righteousness and justice that will come about because of it is the foundation of God's throne.

Thus, on the flip side of Burke's quote, we can say, "All that is necessary for good to triumph is that good men do something." That "something" is what this book is about—

doing the good works of Jesus so that his kingdom will expand and his throne will be established in every nation of this earth.

WHO WILL LEAD?

In his first policy address as attorney general, Alberto Gonzales called trafficking one of the most pernicious moral evils in the world today. As Attorney General Gonzales stated,

> This abomination does not exist only in other lands; it exists right here, on our shores. Today its victims are usually aliens, many of them women and children, smuggled into our country and held in bondage, treated as commodities, stripped of their humanity.[2]

In 2011, CNN launched the Freedom Project, which is their coverage on human trafficking happening around the world. This was a first for them because they are normally just a breaking news network. But they decided to utilize their global resources and influence to expose this evil and influence change. Here is the message from one of their first promotional clips explaining why they started the Freedom Project:

> Around the world, millions of men, women, and children are being bought and sold. Enough is enough. It's time to put an end to modern-day slavery. Today we launch the CNN Freedom Project. All year with CNN's unmatched resources, we go beyond the borders to tackle

slavery head-on, to untangle the criminal web that trades in human life, to give victims a voice, to bring captors to justice, keep government officials to their word. The victims can't walk away and neither will we. It's time to put modern-day slavery out of business, and CNN has joined the fight to bring hope and freedom. The CNN Freedom Project.[3]

I was so inspired when I first saw that. Yet it also left me feeling a bit awkward. Later, I realized why: this should have been the declaration from the church! That should be our message to the world, but we have allowed everyone else to take the lead in this fight for justice, freedom and righteousness. It was then that I gained a stronger conviction of the church's role in this movement.

If we the church are not the preeminent leaders in the fight for justice and in the demonstrations of mercy to the oppressed, then we are allowing the world to look more like Jesus than we do.

We reflect Jesus when we care for the weak, the oppressed, the outcast and the vulnerable. It is time for the church to rise up out of its apathy and slumber to be the leaders and the powerful force we were created to be. We are the light of the world, and where there is light, darkness will flee, for light is always greater than darkness. It is our call to love the oppressed and the outcast, for these are the ones Jesus loves so deeply.

WHAT WILL WE LEAVE BEHIND?

I do not want to leave this great evil as an inheritance to my children's generation. We must rise up and bring an end to injustice, and it must begin today. History records and remembers those who fight for justice. It speaks of men and women who have risen to the challenges of their generation. We honor Harriet Tubman for freeing thousands of slaves through the Underground Railroad. We honor William Wilberforce, the abolitionist who brought an end to the slave trade after forty-six years of fighting. We honor people like them because they fought for freedom. But what if it were happening today? What if you lived in their time period? What would you do? Stand by and do nothing, or join them in their fight?

Something David Batstone wrote woke me up to this situation like nothing else I've read. These were the words that awakened this sleeping soldier:

> There are times to read history, and there are times to make history. We live right now at one of those epic moments in the fight for human freedom. We no longer have to wonder how we might respond to our moment of truth. It is we who are on the stage, and we can change the winds of history with our actions. Future generations will look back to judge our choices and be inspired or disappointed.[4]

You have been given liberty, knowledge, wealth, influence,

position and power for such a time as this. There is a time to read history and there is a time to make history. Now is the time to make history and set the captives free. There is a time and a season for everything, and the time for justice is now.

Church, let's do this!

GROUP DISCUSSION QUESTIONS

- What are some new things you learned through this book study?

- What convicted you the most?

- How will your life be different now?

PRAYER GUIDE

- Pray for a global awakening to happen within the church and that it will lead the way in our pursuit of justice for the oppressed.

- Pray for your church to be a change agent in your community, shining light, being salt, giving love.

- Pray for the injustice of human trafficking to come to an end in our lifetime.

APPENDIX A

Resources for Freedom and Justice

SERMONS

For a series of sermons on human trafficking and justice, visit my website, www.eddiebyun.com

ORGANIZATIONS

Here is a list of some great organizations that are worthy of your prayers and support:

Agape International Missions: http://agapewebsite.org
HOPE Be Restored: www.hopeberestored.org
International Justice Mission (IJM): http://ijm.org
Love 146: www.love146.org
Nightlight International: www.nightlightinternational.com
Not for Sale: www.notforsalecampaign.org
NVADERL www.nvader.org
Polaris Project: www.polarisproject.org
Rahab Ministries Thailand: www.rahabministriesthailand.com
Ratanak International: www.ratanak.org
The A21 Campaign: www.thea21campaign.org

Think Small: http://kidsquestthailand.com
Zoe: http://zoechildren.org

BOOKS

Amazing Grace in the Life of William Wilberforce by John Piper
  and Jonathan Aitken

*Amazing Grace: William Wilberforce and the Heroic Campaign to
  End Slavery* by Eric Metaxas

The Cross of Christ by John Stott

Deepening the Soul for Justice by Bethany H. Hoang

False Justice: Unveiling the Truth About Social Justice by Stuart
  Greaves

Generous Justice: How God's Grace Makes Us Just by Timothy
  Keller

*God in a Brothel: An Undercover Journey into Sex Trafficking and
  Rescue* by Daniel Walker

God, Justice, and Society: Aspects of Law and Legality in the Bible
  by Jonathan Burnside

*Good News About Injustice: A Witness of Courage in a Hurting
  World* by Gary Haugen

The Hole in Our Gospel: What Does God Expect of Us? by
  Richard Stearns

Human Trafficking: A Global Perspective by Louise Shelley

Issues Facing Christians Today by John Stott

*The Just Church: Becoming a Risk-Taking, Justice-Seeking,
  Disciple-Making Congregation* by Jim Martin

Just Courage: God's Great Expedition for the Restless Christian by Gary Haugen

Justice: Rights and Wrongs by Nicholas Wolterstorff

Justice Revolution: When the Church Prays for Justice by Eddie Byun (forthcoming)

The Meeting of the Waters: 7 Global Currents That Will Propel the Future Church by Fritz Kling

The Natashas: The Horrific Inside Story of Slavery, Rape, and Murder in the Global Sex Trade by Victor Malarek

Not for Sale: The Return of the Global Slave Trade—and How We Can Fight It by David Batstone

Sex Trafficking: Inside the Business of Modern Slavery by Siddharth Kara

What Is the Mission of the Church? Making Sense of Social Justice, Shalom, and the Great Commission by Kevin DeYoung and Greg Gilbert

VIDEOS

At the End of Slavery: The Battle for Justice in Our Time (IJM)

Jacob's Story (Unearthed)

Nefarious: Merchant of Souls (Exodus Cry)

The Pink Room (Agape International Missions)

Trade of Innocence

APPS

Free2Work

IJM

Slavery Footprint

CONFERENCES AND TRAINING

Exodus Cry
Agape International Missions
IJM Global Prayer Gathering
The Justice Conference
HOPE Be Restored

INTERNSHIPS

International Justice Mission
Not for Sale
HOPE Be Restored

APPENDIX B

Sample Sermon on Human Trafficking

Title: Stop the Traffick
Key passage: Psalm 10:1-18

INTRODUCTION

Mindy was the youngest child out of six, and though she was only ten years old, she knew it was her Thai duty to provide for her family. With no jobs in her village, she accepted a waitress job in the US through her uncle. When she arrived in LA, her new "boss" took her passport from her for "safekeeping." Without knowing any English, she was totally dependent on her boss. After just two days of work, she was given a new set of clothes that she had to wear. She wasn't comfortable wearing them, so she refused. In anger, her boss violated her, beat her and told her to get dressed. Filled with shame and nowhere to run, her new job of sleeping with men began. After two years in the US, she had only known the inside of hotel rooms, and every three days, she moved into a new city.

I wish this was a rare story, but it's not. It is happening in San Francisco. It is happening in Seoul. It is happening in Shanghai. It is happening in this city. This is the reality of human trafficking today. But thankfully for Mindy, a tip led an undercover officer to have an appointment with her, and he was able to bring her captor to justice and set Mindy free. But sadly, there are many more Mindy's still enslaved even in our city today.

We'll be looking at the reality of modern-day slavery and human trafficking in our sermon for today. It may be a bit emotionally heavy for some, but the basics of this evil need to be established. The stats may shock some of you and disturb others, but it is a reality.

So what is human trafficking? Human trafficking is defined as "the recruitment, harboring, transporting, providing or obtaining of any person for forced labor, slavery or servitude in any industry, including agriculture, construction, prostitution and manufacturing."

Today's text seems as if it were written specifically for this issue. Please open your Bibles to Psalm 10 as we look for ways to stop human trafficking in our day and age.

The first thing we need to do in light of this situation is to:

TURN TO THE LORD AND VENT

Like me, you may have thought that slavery ended a long time ago—like in 1833, when the British Parliament passed the Slavery Abolition Act or in 1865 when the Thirteenth

Amendment to the US Constitution declared slavery to be illegal. But currently, there are more people in slavery now than there ever has been in human history! It is estimated that there are between 20 and 30 million people who are enslaved throughout the world—and even in the US, with over 100,000! Every year, 800,000 to 900,000 human beings are bought, sold or forced across borders. The UN found 700,000 children forced into labor in Indonesia alone. In the European Union, over 120,000 women and children are trafficked into its states. Of those trafficked, 80 percent are female: women and girls. Fifty percent are children—some as young as five years old! Many are between eight and eighteen, and some before they are born!

Sadly, Thailand is a major hub for trafficking. There are 800,000 girls under sixteen years old trafficked to work the bars. Two hundred thousand are under the age of twelve, with red-light districts everywhere.

What are the main reasons people are trafficked in the world today?

1. For work: "bonded labor" or debt labor

2. For sex: they are forced into prostitution or working the bars and brothels

3. Organs

4. Child soldiers: to kill and torture in battles that children were not meant to be in

With these staggering stats, sometimes it looks like the wicked are getting away with evil and God seems distant. When we feel this way, we learn from the psalmist that we need to vent our frustrations to the Lord. Psalm 10:1 says, "Why, O LORD, do you stand far away? Why do you hide yourself in times of trouble?" This passage reads as if the psalmist is looking directly at the trafficking issues in our day. In it, we see the pride of the evildoers in every thought and action.

The passage continues, saying,

> In arrogance the wicked hotly pursue the poor;
>> let them be caught in the schemes that they have
>> devised.
> For the wicked boasts of the desires of his soul,
>> and the one greedy for gain curses and renounces
>> the LORD.
> In the pride of his face the wicked does not seek him;
>> all his thoughts are, "There is no God."
>> (Psalm 10:2-4)

Poverty is what often lures many of these women and children. About 80 percent of those involved in sex trafficking in Thailand are from the northeast part of Thailand. A typical story goes like this: The parents are poor and in desperate need of money. In some parts of Thai culture, the youngest girl is responsible to care of the family. Also, in Thai Buddhism, some believe that if you have five kids and sacrifice one, you'll get more blessing for the rest of your family. But also, they are brought into this system through fraud with the dreams of a better life that awaits them. Others are forced into the sex industry by parents, husbands and even boyfriends.

In the midst of all this evil, it appears that the ones in charge prosper in all they do! Look at verses 5 and 6: "His ways prosper at all times; your judgments are on high, out of his sight; as for all his foes, he puffs at them. He says in his heart, 'I shall not be moved; throughout all generations I shall not meet adversity.'"

This is one of the fastest growing industries in the world. It brings in about seven to ten billion dollars a year! The UN reported that about 60 percent of all men who fly into Bangkok come for sex.

There is a big difference between slavery in the past and slavery today. In the 1800s, slaves were treated as property, so the "owners" at least tried to take care of them. But today, because of how quickly they can be replaced, they are treated like trash.

> His mouth is filled with cursing and deceit and
> > oppression;
> > under his tongue are mischief and iniquity.
> He sits in ambush in the villages;
> > in hiding places he murders the innocent.
> His eyes stealthily watch for the helpless.
> > (Psalm 10:7-8)

This sounds like trafficking today. Traffickers target poor villages because they are most willing to give up their children for money. We see in this that all the plans of the traffickers are evil. "He lurks in ambush like a lion in his thicket; he lurks that he may seize the poor; he seizes the poor when he draws him into his net" (Psalm 10:9).

After capturing them, it is only the beginning of the evil they do. The captors will physically and mentally abuse them. Within the first forty-eight hours, most women and girls are sexually violated to crush any hopes of holding onto their purity and innocence. Soon afterward, they are violated eight to ten times a day every day for years until someone sets them free. But by that time, many have AIDS or STDs and are rejected by their home villages. As a result, the people are crushed.

> The helpless are crushed, sink down,
>   and fall by his might.
> He says in his heart, "God has forgotten,
>   he has hidden his face, he will never see it."
>   (Psalm 10:10-11)

The wicked live with no fear of God. They do not realize that we will all be held accountable before God for the lives that we have lived. We look at all this horror and we should be frustrated, we should vent, but we should vent to the Lord!

After looking at the reality of the situation, our next step must be to . . .

TURN TO THE LORD AND ASK

The greatest action we can do is to pray to the Lord who moves mountains. God moves through prayer. Prayer is the greatest act of faith and warfare we can do each day. "Arise, O LORD; O God, lift up your hand; forget not the afflicted" (Psalm 10:12).

Asking God to "arise" is a call to action. And to ask God to "lift up your hand" is to prepare an army for battle. For example, an army would wait for the hand of their commander to signal the attack. It's saying, "Release your army and unleash your power and authority against the enemy!" That is how we are to pray!

> Why does the wicked renounce God
> > and say in his heart, "You will not call to account"?
> But you do see, for you note mischief and vexation,
> > that you may take it into your hands;
> to you the helpless commits himself;
> > you have been the helper of the fatherless.
> > > (Psalm 10:13-14)

We turn to the Lord because He is the "helper of the fatherless." God's heart is for the weak, helpless and the oppressed, and the true people of God will care for the least of these. Asking God to release his army is also praying for his church to rise up and be the church to the weak, the orphan, the fatherless and the prisoner.

"Break the arm of the wicked and evildoer; call his wickedness to account till you find none" (Psalm 10:15). He is saying, "Destroy the arm of the wicked and make them powerless!" We must pray for justice and freedom. We are to ask God to bring about freedom and peace for the oppressed and dismantle the grip of the oppressors! I am praying each day, asking God to "set every prisoner free in Jesus name!" So when I read stories like the one on Friday where the police in India set free sixty little girls from their slavery in a brothel in India, I rejoice because it is an answer to prayer. Therefore, turn to the Lord and ask him to bring about justice and freedom for the prisoners.

The next thing we must do to help stop the trafficking in the world is to . . .

TURN TO THE LORD AND EXPECT

The LORD is king forever and ever;
>   the nations perish from his land.
O LORD, you hear the desire of the afflicted;
>   you will strengthen their heart; you will incline
>   your ear
to do justice to the fatherless and the oppressed,
>   so that man who is of the earth may strike terror no
>   more. (Psalm 10:16-18)

Sometimes hearing these stats and stories can be discouraging, making us want to give up before we even start. But never let your focus remain on the mountains. Instead, we must focus on the God who created the mountains and who is greater than the mountains. We fix our eyes on Jesus, the good king who protects his people, provides for his people and rules in justice.

We must expect God to move and to act on behalf of those he loves. We must expect miracles to happen, and we must expect justice. "O LORD, you hear the desire of the afflicted; you will strengthen their heart; you will incline your ear to do justice to the fatherless and the oppressed, so that man who is of the earth may strike terror no more" (Psalm 10:17-18).

God also gives in response to expectations and faith. When we expect great things from our great God, great things will happen!

And finally, in order to stop trafficking, we must . . .

TURN TO THE LORD AND ACT

After we vent to the Lord, ask of the Lord for freedom and expect him to work, we must then turn to the Lord (meaning, stay in prayer) but also act on behalf of the Lord, for a primary means of accomplishing justice is through his people. "For I the LORD love justice" (Isaiah 61:8).

What is justice to God? Our idea of injustice in the world is a bit different from the Bible's idea. I like how Gary Haugen puts it. We think getting cut off on the street while driving is an injustice. Or when we're at the grocery store with three items in the 10-items-or-less express lane and the person in front of us has fifteen items. You know because you counted. "Injustice!" we cry out.

But according to God, injustice is an abuse of power, where

the strong take from the weak and deny rights of life, liberty and dignity. Injustice is when a police officer in Thailand who makes only sixty dollars per month will allow women and children to be abused and kidnapped because the pimp will pay him off to look the other way. God hates injustice and wants it to stop! God hates seeing the poor exploited, children abused and women imprisoned! But until Christ returns, we are God's plan for justice in the world.

> He has told you, O man, what is good;
>> and what does the LORD require of you
> but to do justice, and to love kindness,
>> and to walk humbly with your God? (Micah 6:8)

> Woe to you, scribes and Pharisees, hypocrites! For you tithe mint and dill and cumin, and have neglected the weightier matters of the law: justice and mercy and faithfulness. These you ought to have done, without neglecting the others. (Matthew 23:23)

How will the oppressed and suffering see the goodness of God? Through his body, his church. We are his hands that will hold them, his arms that will embrace them and his defense that will fight for them! You are the light of the world. You are the salt of the earth. God is against injustice, so when we fight for justice, we are fighting for the things of God's heart and therefore God fights with us and for us.

We must act. As the people of God, on behalf of God.

Edmund Burke said, "All that is necessary for the triumph of evil is that good men do nothing." We must be Christ to them!

Last winter, our mission team met an amazing woman named Jenny at an aftercare center. She was always so full of laughter, and though she was a grandmother, she literally played around like a kid. She would play jokes on other people, pulling chairs out from under them. She just loved joking around with others. Then one of the workers at the aftercare center took me aside and asked if I knew why she was acting like a child. It was because she was abused and enslaved since she was a little girl. She had lost her childhood. She hadn't played with friends. She hadn't gone to school. She had men abusing her eight to ten times a day for decades. But now she is free, Christ is restoring her, and she is able to laugh and joke like a child again. Only Jesus Christ can restore the years that the locusts have eaten away. And his method to reach them is his body—you and me. That is why we are doing this. Because millions of babies, little kids and teenage girls are waiting for God to show up in the form of his church and set them free.

That is why we are launching this justice ministry in our church, because this is what burdens the heart of God. This is the core of what the gospel is about. We were slaves trapped in sin, but Jesus, our great abolitionist, came to set us free!

But thanks be to God, that you who were once slaves of sin have become obedient from the heart to the standard of teaching to which you were committed, and, having been set free from sin, have become slaves of righteousness. (Romans 6:17-18)

This fight for their freedom is a physical expression of what the gospel seeks to do in every area of our lives. It is for freedom Christ set us free. And that is why you have your freedom, your finances and your faith—so that the purposes of God's heart might be accomplished through his children. Through you!

So what can we do? Here are some practical next steps to take.

Become aware. Come to the conference we will have later this month on trafficking. Read books on this issue. Become familiar with what is happening in this country and around the world.

Stay in prayer. Begin praying for freedom for the enslaved. Pray for ministries that fight for their freedom. Pray for this city and for those who are enslaved in our own backyards, that they might be freed and healed, physically and spiritually.

Give of your resources. Give to some great organizations that are also fighting on the frontlines of this battle. Go on some of our short-term missions "freedom projects" that focus on this issue. Volunteer your services at some of these aftercare centers.

CONCLUSION

History records and remembers those who fight for justice. History tells of men and women who have risen to the challenge. We honor Harriet Tubman for the role she played in freeing thousands of slaves through the Underground Railroad. History honors William Wilberforce, the abolitionist who brought an end to the slave trade after forty-six years of fighting. History honors them because they fought for freedom. But what if it were happening today? What if you lived in their time period? What would you do? Stand by and do nothing, or join them in their fight? History records and remembers those who fight for justice.

Something David Batstone said woke me up to this situation like nothing else I've read on this issue. These were the words that awakened this sleeping soldier:

> There are times to read history, and there are times to make history. We live right now at one of those epic moments in the fight for human freedom. We no longer have to wonder how we might respond to our moment of truth. It is we who are on the stage, and we can change the winds of history with our actions. Future generations will look back to judge our choices and be inspired or disappointed.[1]

You have been given liberty, knowledge, wealth and influence for such a time as this. There is a time to read history, and there's a time to make history. Now is the time to make history and set the captives free. Let's do this, church!

Let's pray.

APPENDIX C

Case Study on Korea

A GLIMPSE INTO SOUTH KOREA'S DOMESTIC AND INTERNATIONAL HUMAN TRAFFICKING ISSUES

Hope Be Restored Research Team[1]

INTRODUCTION

Human trafficking is a form of modern-day slavery. As of 2012, the International Labor Office (ILO) reports that approximately 20 million people are victims of human trafficking.[2] There are 161 countries reportedly affected by human trafficking, either by being a source, transit or destination country.[3] Additionally, the ILO reports that 4.5 million people are trafficked with the intent of being used for sexual exploitation.[4] An overwhelming majority of these victims end up in the sex industry in the Pacific and Asia.[5] These statistics have caused Hope Be Restored, a Seoul-based organization, to take a stand against this injustice and pursue the abolishment of human trafficking both in and out of South Korea.

As defined by the United Nations (UN), human trafficking

involves any act of recruiting, transporting, transferring, harboring or receiving a person through a use of force, coercion or other means, for the purpose of exploiting them.[6] Hope Be Restored is working under this definition of human trafficking and, for the purpose of clarification, incorporating prostitution—whether voluntary or forced—into our data. Though slightly controversial, the admittance of prostitution is crucial because those who are trafficked in and out of South Korea are primarily involved in the sex industry. Differentiating voluntary and forced prostitution is nearly impossible due to the nature of the industry. Therefore, since prostitution is illegal in South Korea, Hope Be Restored has chosen to include all data associated with prostitution.

This report will primarily focus on three major aspects of South Korea's human trafficking network and its sex industry. These focuses are:

- Koreans trafficked out of South Korea
- Foreigners trafficked into South Korea
- Koreans trafficked within South Korea

A BRIEF HISTORY OF HUMAN TRAFFICKING IN AND OUT OF SOUTH KOREA

In the twentieth century, Korea was the country of origin for many migrant workers around the world. Koreans sought migrant work in pursuit of opportunity and highly valued foreign currency. The sex industry was one of its exports, sending women to conflict zones so they could offer their services to military personnel, largely servicing US soldiers fighting in the Vietnam War.[7]

In the 1990s, due to the boom in the Korean economy, more money than ever began to flow through the country. This increase in capital brought a higher standard of living and an increase in expendable income, an unimaginable luxury of ages past. With this economic boost, the roles of migrant workers reversed—instead of flowing out of the country, they began to flow in. As of 1996, Korea has "changed from a country of origin for international sex trafficking in women to become a host country."[8] The increase in demand generated a steady supply and vice versa, confirming that the Korean sex industry is a market-based economy that exists on the principle of supply and demand with high profits and little risk. Thus, the sex industry in South Korea is highly profitable and a strong harvesting ground for imported and exported sex workers.

KOREANS TRAFFICKED OUT OF SOUTH KOREA

South Korean women are reported to be the most trafficked nationals into the US, Japan and Australia. The countries are rated on a 4 Tier scale—Tier 1 being the highest—according to how they comply with the Trafficking Victims Protection Act (2000) passed by the US Department of State.

United States. The US is ranked as a Tier 1 country in the

US Department of State's TIP 2012 report.[9] In the US Attorney General's report for FY2005, it says, "The highest populations of victims originated in Korea (23.5%), Thailand (11.7%), Peru (10.0%), and Mexico (9.6%)," but this is within the context of certification of victims under the TVPA (Trafficking Victims Protection Act of 2000).[10] Korea was the biggest population for those victims who were reported, then subsequently certified. It cannot be said how good this measure is as an indication of the overall situation. Furthermore, the same report for 2010 showed that Korea had dropped to fourth place.

The United States views prostitution as illegal and takes legal action to eradicate the sex industry. But the US is one of the largest destinations for Korean trafficking. As of 2007, there are approximately 300,000 Koreans illegally in the US according to the US Office of Immigration Statistics.[11] The areas that have the largest number of Korean-operated sex establishments are the Northeastern US, Dallas, San Francisco and Los Angeles.[12] These areas are densely populated with illegal Koreans and have been the focus of many FBI investigations regarding the sex industry. In LA alone, there is an estimated total of 10,000 Korean women working in the sex industry.[13]

The US law enforcement reported that in the major areas, such as LA and San Francisco, there was an estimate of 345 venues owned by Koreans that offered sexual services.[14] According to Barry Tang, an Immigration and Customs Enforcement attached with the US Department of Homeland

Security in South Korea, "There's a highly organized logical network between Korea and the United States with recruiters, brokers, intermediaries, taxi drivers, and madams."[15] Though it is extremely difficult to have a firm number on how many Koreans are actually trafficked into the US for the purpose of sexual exploitation, it is safe to assume that no matter the exact number, thousands of Koreans are being sexually exploited in the US annually.

CASE STUDY

Sex trafficking victims rarely receive the opportunity to publicly tell their story. Therefore, when the *San Francisco Gate* did a three-part series on a Korean college student, You Mi Kim, who revealed she had been smuggled into California by sex traffickers, people began to listen.[16]

Kim came from a poor family, but when she went to college and was offered a credit card, she saw the opportunity to impress her friends. She spent lavishly on clothes and cosmetics and entertaining her newfound friends, and was ten thousand dollars in debt after a year. The credit card company cut off her credit, and she was obliged to take out loans from loan sharks at 25 percent to repay the debt. She dropped out of college and found work, but even so her spending behavior did not change. She acquired another credit card to pay back the debt and continued to go to the loans sharks. A year later, she was forty thousand dollars in debt.

She considered prostituting herself in bars to repay the

mounting debt, but she could not stomach it and she thought her prayers had been answered when she saw an internet ad promising, "Work in an American room salon. Make ten thousand dollars a month. Very gentle. No touching. No second round."[17] She figured she could work for six months and come back to re-enroll in college. As she didn't have a passport or a visa, the agent said she would have to pay seven thousand dollars in travel expenses, which she could repay with her earnings. She was unsure, but desperate to be freed of her debt, she agreed.

Unexpectedly, her flight was bound for Mexico. Her handlers explained that it was because she didn't have a visa and it was easier to get into the US this way. She transferred to Tijuana and was driven across the border, eventually to arrive in Los Angeles. There, her new boss informed her that her travel expenses had come to eleven thousand dollars. Exhausted from a week of nerve-wracking travel, she agreed.

Her boss drove her to several room salons for job interviews, but she was turned down at all of them. In the end, he offered her an ultimatum: pay back the money she owed for her travel and accommodation expenses or work for his wife's outcall service as a prostitute. With her forty thousand dollars of debt waiting for her at home, she had no choice but to accept. On her first day she was called out three times but she did not keep any of the money—half went to paying her debt and the other half went to the outcall service.

She was awkward and inexperienced so she couldn't keep

her customers, and after two months she still owed six thousand dollars to her traffickers. They got impatient and sold her on for seventy-two hundred dollars. Kim ended up in a brothel in a residential neighborhood. At the end of her twelve-hour shift on her first day there, she had had sex with fourteen men. After three months of being bounced around from one establishment to another in LA, she was free of her debt to the traffickers, but she still had the debt in Korea, and she had incurred ten thousand dollars in legal fees when she was arrested for prostitution. She was free, but she could not leave. She had no choice but to carry on, and she moved to San Francisco where the pay was better.

For the next four months she would service more than twelve men a day, six days a week, in San Francisco's notorious Tenderloin district. She became unrecognizable as a person. She went from being shy and nervous to bouncy and playful with her customers, hoping to get repeat customers who believed she enjoyed spending time with them. The more work she got, the faster she could get herself out of the hole. And it worked. After four months, she had paid off her all her debts in the US and Korea. It was over.

But she couldn't go home. The shame of what she had done and the trouble she had caused her family prevented her from returning to Korea. She received a T-1 visa, and she currently resides in San Francisco working as a waitress. She finds it difficult to make friends, and she keeps her face down in public in case one of her clients recognizes her. She has lingering health problems and the gynecologist has told her that she has a high chance of contracting cervical cancer. She is twenty-three years old.

Japan. Prostitution is illegal in Japan, but it is still tolerated. Japan was ranked as a Tier 2 country in the US Department of State's TIP 2012 report.[18] There are from 130,000 to 150,000 foreign women in Japan's $83 billion sex industry.[19] According to the Japanese Ministry of Justice, there are estimated to be 6,000 to 7,000 Koreans documented to be working in the sex industry under the entertainment visa.[20] Entertainment visas are the primary way in which foreign women are brought into countries in order to cover up the sex industry. According to Polaris Project Japan's hotline, "About 30% of S.O.S calls made to the hotline since 2005 were by Koreans, making them the most targeted foreign victims."[21]

Australia. Australia was ranked as a Tier 1 country in the US Department of State's TIP 2012 report.[22] Figures and studies show that the majority of trafficked people are being brought in from Asian countries and a large part from South Korea, specifically. According to one study, "Between the 2003-04 and 2009-10 financial years . . . 26% [of trafficked victims to the United States] involved South Korean nationals."[23] Unfortunately, there is not much solid research on specific numbers of cases of human trafficking in Australia, but most sources claim a relatively low number. This is largely due to the fact that in Australia, according to the Prostitution Act of 1992, prostitution is considered legal and does not fall under what they consider to be human trafficking. Under the same Act, it is also stated that all brothels and the people involved must be registered with the government.[24]

However, if the woman does identify herself as being a victim of human trafficking specifically, the Australian government provides many options in the form of aid and protection. For example, as of July 2009, victims are offered an opportunity to acquire a Witness Protection visa (which is permanent and would also encompass their family) given that they help in the prosecution of criminals within the industry.[25]

FOREIGNERS TRAFFICKED INTO SOUTH KOREA

It is possible that the apex of the issue of Koreans trafficking foreigners into Korea lies in the discrepancies of the issuance and application of the E-6 visa. This specific visa issued to foreigners is labeled the "Arts/Entertainment" visa. This is issued with the understanding that recipients are in Korea to pursue careers within that realm. However, it has often been the case that traffickers have sought and received this visa for individuals whom they promised entertainment careers (in some cases in the K-pop industry) and upon arrival, said individuals were forced into sexual servitude and coerced by their visa situation, which requires participation in the "arts" as the only means of making money while in the country.

This first became an issue with the importing of Russian women, mostly to camp towns outside of US army bases; however, in 2003 the South Korean government stopped issuing the E-6 visa to the Russian women. Recently, there has been a noticed increase in the issuance of the E-6 visa, only this time to Filipino woman. The book *Exposing the Price Tag* remarks, "Since [2003], a growing number of Filipino women have been issued the same E-6 visa to gain entry to Korea, replacing Russian dancers."[26] Furthermore, a recent article in the *Korea Times* states that while there has been a pleasant restriction to the E-6 visa since the time it was being used to bring Russian women over to Korea, it is now being used to authorize Filipino women to work the "juicy bars" near these army bases. These are run off of the basis that soldiers buy glasses of juice to spend time, flirt and dance with the women. "Those women who fail to meet a quota for juice sales are often subject to 'bar fines,' meaning they are told to sell their body to account for the shortfall."[27] This highlights the crux of the issue with the E-6 visa: with the requisite to obtain the visa being "for those seeking to make profit with performance" the definition of what performance entails is unnecessarily ambiguous. It is clear that until the definition is clarified as to what qualifies as appropriate "performance," this incongruity will enable the genre of exploitation.

There were 4,970 E-6 visa holders in Korea in 2009—77 percent of them were women.[28] The Korean Ministry of Culture, Sports and Tourism (MCST—the government ministry which oversees the E-6 visa), has been "criticized for automatically approving visa applicants through local entertainment companies. For example, it does not monitor workplaces employing E-6 workers."[29] This is not a new situation. Five years earlier, the ILO's 2004 report "Human Trafficking for Sexual Exploitation in Japan" said that the Japanese Immigration Bureau "plans to review the requirements for the Entertainment Visa and/or examine more closely the qualifications of applicants as entertainers."[30] While it cannot be said that the Korean government has abetted the trafficking of entertainers, certainly its negligence in screening the applicants for E-6 visas, as it would do stringently for any other visa application, is noteworthy.

KOREANS TRAFFICKED WITHIN SOUTH KOREA

Though many hail from other nations, a large part of the 270,000 prostitutes in Korea are Korean.[31] While the reasons for their entry into the industry may vary, most are deceived by friends or pimps, and others are "sold" because of debt.[32] Of these women, 80 percent are victims of physical violence— seven out of ten having attempted suicide.[33] With 94 million cases of prostitution occurring every year, prostitution is a fourteen-trillion-won industry in Korea alone.[34]

The 2004 Act on the Prevention of Sexual Traffic and Protection of Victims changed the face of the prostitution industry in Korea. The number of prostituted women fell from 330,000 in 2002 to 270,000 by 2007, and the value of the industry plunged from over twenty-four trillion won in 2002 to fourteen trillion won in 2007.[35] It is surmised, however, that the 2004 Act served to drive prostitution further underground, with internet prostitution seeing a 50 percent increase over the same period. Reinvented brothels run out of offices, and residential locations are said to have seen a meteoric rise but are virtually untraceable.

At the ground level, enforcement of the Act is key. The Lee Myung-bak administration, which took office in 2009, has shown a hawkish attitude toward prostitution by cutting funding for shelters for prostituted women and relaxing police enforcement. A prostituted woman working in a red-light district (RLD) says, "I know the law has changed, but it doesn't have any real meaning."[36] A support center for prostituted women stated, "There were about 80 establishments here before 2004 Act, . . . and when the police started enforcing the law, the number dropped to about 50. Now it's back up to 60 or 70."[37]

The workers in Korean RLDs are primarily teenage runaways. Runaways often become targets for prostitution. Statistics state:[38]

- There are an estimated 200,000 runaways in Korea.

- A quarter of all runaway girls admit to have given sexual favors for money.

- The average age of running away from home for the first time is thirteen.

- Runaways are getting younger: between 2010 and 2011, the total number of reported runaways increased by 44 percent, but the number of runaways under thirteen increased by 148 percent.

CASE STUDY

The story below is an actual account taken from the book *Exposing the Price Tag*. Yujin Lee was lured into the trafficking industry when her father's health took a turn for the worse and she felt obligated to help support her family. Going to a fortune teller, she learned that she could make good money at a dabang[39] and that she would even gain a 2,000,000 won (one month's salary) advance payment. She learned after starting that the job required sexual intercourse, but she complied because she needed the money desperately. She says:

> I could not bear it, so when the first month was over, I ran away. The owner of Byul Dabang called me saying, "How could you leave without telling me? It has been fifteen days since you left, so you owe me damages of 2,300,000 won. Combined with your other debts, the total you now owe me is 5,600,000 won. If you want to quit, you'd better pay me 5,600,000 won." I said, "I'm sorry for leaving without saying anything, but I received one month's payment of 2,000,000 won as an advance payment, and I worked for a month. How could I owe you 5,600,000 won?" The owner threatened me. "If you don't bring the money, I will sue you for fraud and tell your parents." I knew this was unfair, but I was so afraid that my parents would find out.[40]

Lee's story goes on to detail her movement from dabang to dabang, the abusive treatment she received from owners and customers alike, her virtual imprisonment to the industry, and her ever-increasing debt, which eventually amounted to an astounding 16,000,000 won. Unfortunately, Lee's story is not unique; like Kim in San Francisco, this method of debt incursion is a very common form of manipulation to keep young Korean women hostage in the sex trade.

CONCLUSION

Nestled nicely between Southeast Asia and North America, South Korea is an ideal hub across one of the world's largest human trafficking routes. Whether as traffickers, pimps or victims, Koreans are certainly playing an active role in human trafficking internationally and domestically. Many Korean women, such as Kim and Lee, have found themselves in financial trouble and lured into prostitution under false pretenses while others have turned to it in desperation. Through generous distribution and trouble-free access to E-6 visas, foreigners are easily brought into Korea and lost within a convoluted and constantly changing system.

Korea is ranked as a Tier 1 country on the US Department of State's TIP report.[41] The general rates of prostitution have been reportedly lower over the last few years in South Korea; however, these positive claims are not particularly evident on the streets. This leaves observers with the impression that the Korean government is simply complying to international standards without actually enforcing any tangible reforms to eradicate and prevent human trafficking and prostitution within its borders. An example of this situation can be seen in Korea's efforts against prostitution. Though prostitution is considered illegal and there are penalties for violators, there are few firm attempts at enforcement. This lack of enforcement has allowed the industry to thrive within and out of Korea.

The global sex industry and human trafficking go hand-in-hand—without one, the other cannot live, and vice versa. This is the same for the supply and demand. In order to begin combating this difficult issue there needs to be a lower demand and a cut in supply. Therefore, international awareness and government assertiveness are key to this issue and the only true hope for abolishment. This report simply begins to broach this topic. Hope Be Restored seeks to open the dialogue and continually pursue the eradication of human trafficking.

For more information regarding Hope Be Restored, please visit hopeberestored.org.

ACKNOWLEDGMENTS

Thank you, Jesus, for your amazing grace in saving me and the honor you give me of serving your people and preaching your gospel.

Thank you, Hyun, for being so gracious, loving and faithful. You are an amazing wife and mother. Thank you to my parents for their love and support and for cheering me on through every season of my life.

Thank you, Al Hsu and the amazing team at IVP, for believing in this project. Thank you, Charse Yun, for lending your gifts of editing and for detail to help with this project.

Thank you to my pastoral and administrative staff at Onnuri English Ministry: Joel Yoon, Michael Lee, Isaac Surh, Daniel Park, Buri Suk, Mira Ahn, Estella Kang, JC Park, Mike Kim, Jane Kim, Eunji Kim, Andy Hodges, David Chung, Eunice Yun, Don Sutton, Stephanie Kim, Liz Linssen, Lisa Pak, Johnny Lee, Sonia Yim, Sophia Ha, Hermann Kim, Grace

Kim, Daniel Im and Christina Im. Thank you to the amazing intercessors of OEM, especially Hannah Biggs, Kate Derbisire, Iman Lu, Christine Kim, Judy Kim, Izabel Orendain, Jonathan Miller, Mira Miller, Elisa Lee, Gladys Figueroa, Mimi Song, Richard Biggs, Julie Brown, Ludy Ko and Elizabeth Lee. Thank you to my OEM family for taking these steps of faith with me. To our elders and deacons, I love you all.

Thank you to the HOPE Be Restored team for pioneering this justice ministry for South Korea. Thank you Jonathan English, Gracie Kim and Jacob Bennett. Thank you Onnuri Community Church, Pastor Ha Yong Jo, Pastor Jae Hoon Lee, the Onnuri Women's Ministry, CGNTV, the Christian CEO Forum, Elder Philip Choi and Duranno Publishing. Thank you to the faculty, staff and students of Torch Trinity Graduate University, especially to my students who pioneered our Freedom and Justice course together. Thank you to all the AIM pastors for their love and support, especially David and Judy Hwang, Christian and Erin Lee, and Doug Park. Thank you Handong Global University, Handong International Law School, Christ Bible Institute of Japan and New Life Worship.

Thank you David Batstone and the Not for Sale family, who opened my eyes to the injustice of human trafficking. Thank you to my fellow abolitionists Benji Nolot, Tara Teng, Don Brewster, Annie Dieselberg, Nightlight International, Rahab Ministries, Thailand, Exodus Cry, IJM, Ratanak, Unearthed, Voice of the Voiceless, Ecogender, Durebang, Dashihamke, Saenal, Women's Hope Center and House of Hope for partnering together in our fight for freedom and justice in Korea and across the nations. Thank you Eddie Kim, Pat Yoon, KJ Lee, Bobby Lee, Midwest Youth Group, Philadelphia Church of Vancouver. Thank you also to Jayesslee, Brian Joo, Danny Jung, Tim Hwang and Jennifer Chung for supporting our justice conferences with your talents.

NOTES

CHAPTER 1: GOD'S PASSION FOR JUSTICE IN HIS WORLD

[1]Timothy Keller, *Generous Justice: How God's Grace Makes Us Just* (New York: Riverhead Books, 2012), p. 2.

[2]Ibid., p. 3.

[3]Gary Haugen, *Good News About Injustice: A Witness of Courage in a Hurting World* (Downers Grove, IL: InterVarsity Press, 2009), p. 71.

[4]Keller, *Generous Justice*, p. 2.

[5]Kevin DeYoung, *Don't Call It a Comeback: The Old Faith for a New Day* (Wheaton, IL: Crossway, 2011), p. 156.

[6]Bethany H. Hoang, *Deepening the Soul for Justice,* Urbana Onward (Downers Grove, IL: InterVarsity Press, 2012), p. 24.

CHAPTER 2: WHERE IS THE JUSTICE OF GOD?

[1]Alan E. Lewis, *Between Cross and Resurrection: A Theology of Holy Saturday* (Grand Rapids: Eerdmans, 2003), p. 323.

[2]J. I. Packer, *Knowing God* (Downers Grove, IL: InterVarsity Press, 1993), p. 125.

[3]John Stott, *The Cross of Christ* (Downers Grove, IL: InterVarsity Press, 2006), p. 207.

[4]Michael D. Williams, *Far as the Curse Is Found: The Covenant Story of Redemption* (Phillipsburg, NJ: P & R Publishing, 2005), p. 269.

CHAPTER 3: EXPOSING THE DARKNESS OF MODERN-DAY SLAVERY

[1]David Batstone, *Not for Sale: The Return of the Global Slave Trade—and How We Can Fight It* (San Francisco: HarperOne, 2010), p. 1.

[2]Ibid., p. 3.

[3]Louise Shelley, *Human Trafficking: A Global Perspective of Modern Day Human Trafficking and Sex Slavery* (New York: Cambridge University Press, 2010), p. 5.

[4]Ibid.

[5]Ibid., p. 2.

[6]See www.unodc.org/unodc/en/human-trafficking/what-is-human-trafficking.html?ref=menuside.

[7]See "What Is Modern Slavery?" U.S. Department of State, www.state.gov/j/tip/what/index.htm.

[8]See Kevin Bales, *Understanding Global Slavery* (Los Angeles: University of California Press, 2005), p. 150.

[9]Shelley, *Human Trafficking,* p. 64.

[10]Ibid., p. 2.

[11]Ibid., p. 64.

[12]Ibid., p. 5. See also "What Is Modern Slavery?" U.S. Department of State, www.state.gov/j/tip/what/index.htm.

[13]Bales, *Understanding Global Slavery,* p. 150. See also www.theguardian.com/world/2012/may/27/kidney-trade-illegal-operations-who.

[14]Shelley, *Human Trafficking,* p. 14.

[15]Daniel Walker, *God in a Brothel: An Undercover Journey into Sex Trafficking and Rescue* (Downers Grove, IL: InterVarsity Press, 2011), p. 17. See also "What Is Modern Slavery?" U.S. Department of State, www.state.gov/j/tip/what/index.htm.

[16]Shelley, *Human Trafficking*, p. 53.

[17]See www.justice.gov/archive/ag/annualreports/tr2006/agreport humantrafficing2006.pdf.

[18]Shelley, *Human Trafficking*, p. 52.

[19]See www.polarisproject.org/human-trafficking/overview/the-victims.

[20]Shelley, *Human Trafficking*, p. 51.

[21]Ibid., p. 57.

[22]Ibid., pp. 2-3.

[23]Ibid., p. 16.

[24]Ibid., p. 7.

[25]From a presentation by Don Brewster on Cambodia at my church.

CHAPTER 4: WHY THE CHURCH MUST LEAD

[1]Kevin DeYoung and Greg Gilbert, *What Is the Mission of the Church? Making Sense of Social Justice, Shalom, and the Great Commission* (Wheaton, IL: Crossway, 2011), p. 225.

[2]John Stott, *Issues Facing Christians Today* (Grand Rapids: Zondervan, 2006), p. 67.

[3]Ibid., p. 26 (Kindle ed.).

[4]See www.cslewisinstitute.org/William_Wilberforce_FullArticle, p. 4.

[5]John Piper, *Amazing Grace in the Life of William Wilberforce* (Wheaton, IL: Crossway, 2007), p. 41 (Kindle edition).

[6]Fritz Kling, *The Meeting of the Waters: 7 Global Currents That Will Propel the Future Church* (Colorado Springs: David C. Cook, 2010), p. 41.

[7]Ibid., p. 28.

CHAPTER 5: WHAT THE CHURCH CAN DO

[1]David Batstone, *Not for Sale: The Return of the Global Slave Trade—*

and How We Can Fight It (San Francisco: HarperOne, 2010), p. 1.

[2]Bethany Hoang, *Deepening the Soul for Justice,* Urbana Onward (Downers Grove, IL: InterVarsity Press, 2012), p. 7.

[3]Gary Haugen, *Just Courage: God's Great Expedition for the Restless Christian* (Downers Grove, IL: InterVarsity Press, 2008), p. 23.

[4]Testimony taken from AIM's website: http://agapewebsite.org/projects/lords-gym.

[5]Ibid.

CONCLUSION

[1]See http://thegospelcoalition.org/blogs/tgc/2013/08/09/9-things-you-should-know-about-human-trafficking.

[2]"Attorney General's Annual Report to Congress on U.S. Government Activities to Combat Trafficking in Persons Fiscal Year 2005," U.S. Department of Justice, 2006, p. 41. See www.justice.gov/archive/ag/annualreports/tr2006/agreporthumantrafficing2006.pdf.

[3]The first commercial advertising CNN's Freedom Project, http://youtu.be/glm54PrNNxA.

[4]David Batstone, *Not for Sale: The Return of the Global Slave Trade— and How We Can Fight It* (San Francisco: HarperOne, 2010) p. 17.

APPENDIX B: SAMPLE SERMON ON HUMAN TRAFFICKING

[1]David Batstone, *Not for Sale: The Return of the Global Slave Trade— and How We Can Fight It* (San Francisco: HarperOne, 2010) p. 17.

APPENDIX C: CASE STUDY ON KOREA

[1]Contributors: Genevieve Pierce, Cynthia Goss, Richard Biggs, Ben Spink, Michelle Constantine and Rebekah McNay. Editing/Formatting: Genevieve Pierce and Cynthia Goss.

[2]"ILO 2012 Global Estimate of Forced Labour," International

Labour Office, 2012, www.ilo.org, accessed September 1, 2012.

[3]"Human Trafficking: The Facts," UN Global Initiative to Fight Human Trafficking, 2007, www.ungift.org, accessed August 29, 2012.

[4]"ILO 2012 Global Estimate of Forced Labour," International Labour Office, 2012, www.ilo.org, accessed September 1, 2012.

[5]Ibid.

[6]"Human trafficking," United Nations, www.unodc.org, accessed August 28, 2012.

[7]Seol Dong-Hoon, "International Sex Trafficking in Women in Korea: Its Causes, Consequences and Countermeasures," *Asian Center for Women's Studies* 10, no. 2 (2004): 8.

[8]Ibid.

[9]"Trafficking in Persons Report—2012," US Department of State, 2012, www.state.gov/j/tip/rls/tiprpt/2012, accessed August 29, 2012.

[10]"Attorney General's Annual Report to Congress on U.S. Government Activities to Combat Trafficking in Persons Fiscal Year 2005," US Department of Justice, 2006, p. 6.

[11]Ibid., p. 12.

[12]Tim Lim, "The Dynamics of Trafficking, Smuggling and Prostitution: An Analysis of Korean Women in the U.S. Commercial Sex Industry," University of California, Los Angeles, 2008, p. 9.

[13]Ibid., p. 10.

[14]Ibid., p. 9.

[15]Meredith May, "The Diary of a Sex Slave: Part 1," *San Francisco Gate,* October 6, 2006, www.sfgate.com/news/article/SEX-TRAFFICKING-San-Francisco-Is-A-Major-Center-2468554.php, accessed September 24, 2012.

[16]Ibid.

[17]Ibid.

[18]"Trafficking in Persons Report—2012," US Department of State, 2012, www.state.gov/j/tip/rls/tiprpt/2012, accessed August 29, 2012.

[19]Donna M, Hughes, "The Demand for Victims of Sex Trafficking," Women's Studies, University of Rhode Island 2005, p. 14.

[20]Ibid.

[21]Sim Guk-by, "Korean Victims of Sex Trafficking in Japan Receive Renewed Attention," *Korean Herald,* June 21, 2012, http://view.koreaherald.com/kh/view.php?ud=20120621001188&cpv=0, accessed September 24, 2012.

[22]"Trafficking in Persons Report—2012," US Department of State, 2012, www.state.gov/j/tip/rls/tiprpt/2012, accessed August 29, 2012.

[23]"Human Trafficking Working Group—Statistics and Other Data," The University of Queensland, 2011, www.law.uq.edu.au/human-trafficking-statistics, accessed September 12, 2011.

[24]"Republication of the Prostitution Act of 1992," ACT Parliamentary Counsel, Australian Government, December 12, 2011, www.legislation.act.gov.au/a/1992-64/current/pdf/1992-64.pdf, accessed September 9, 2012.

[25]"Human Trafficking to Australia: A Research Challenge," Australian Institute of Criminology, June 2007, http://aic.gov.au/documents/7/B/A/%7B7BA2B075-9282-4331-98A6-14080E701B2B%7Dtandi338.pdf, accessed September 13, 2011.

[26]Dassi Hamkke Center, *Exposing the Price Tag* (Seoul, 2012), p. 125.

[27]"Fight to End Trafficking Near US Bases in Korea," *Korea Times,* February 27, 2012, www.koreatimes.co.kr, accessed March 1, 2012.

[28]"Disposable Labour: Rights of Migrant Workers in South Korea," *Amnesty International* (2009): 80.

[29]Ibid.

[30]"Human Trafficking for Sexual Exploitation in Japan," International Labour Office, 2004, www.ilo.org, accessed September 1, 2012.

[31]"Survey of the National Status of Sex Trafficking," *Ministry of Gender Equality and Family (MOGEF)* (2007): xvii.

[32]"Survey of the National Status of Sex Trafficking," *MOGEF* (2010): 8.

[33]"Their Choice," promotional video for prostitution prevention campaign, *MOGEF* (2012).

[34]"Survey of the National Status of Sex Trafficking," *MOGEF* (2007): xix.

[35]Ibid., p. xxii.

[36]Hankyoreh, "14 Years in Hell," *Hani Online* (Korea), December 12, 2011, http://h21.hani.co.kr/arti/society/society_general/30944 .html, accessed October 1, 2012.

[37]Ibid.

[38]"Runaway families—Dangerous Cohabitation," *Chu Cheog 60bun,* (추적60분—*60 Minute Investigation*), KBS, aired July 11, 2012, www.kbs.co.kr/2tv/sisa/chu60/vod/1959367_879.html, accessed September 3, 2012.

[39]Dabangs are teahouses specializing in home delivery that are notorious for providing sexual service. Since they are officially categorized as a restaurant or entertainment business and can legally hire teenagers, dabangs are a common entry point into the sex trade for underage girls (*Exposing the Price Tag,* p. 145).

[40]Ibid., pp. 49-50.

[41]"Trafficking in Persons Report—2012," US Department of State, 2012, www.state.gov/j/tip/rls/tiprpt/2012, accessed August 29, 2012.